INTERNET EXPLORER 4
in easy steps

Mary Lojkine

COMPUTER STEP

In easy steps is an imprint of Computer Step
Southfield Road . Southam
Warwickshire CV33 OFB . England

Tel: 01926 817999 Fax: 01926 817005
http://www.computerstep.com

Notice of Liability
Every effort has been made to ensure that this book contains accurate
and current information. However, Computer Step and the author shall
not be liable for any loss or damage suffered by readers as a result of
any information contained herein.

Trademarks
All trademarks are acknowledged as belonging to their respective
companies.

Printed and bound in the United Kingdom

ISBN 1-874029-84-9

Contents

7   Internet security   103

8   Subscriptions and Channels   113

9   The Active Desktop   127

Chapter One

Getting started

Before you can make use of Internet Explorer, you need to get connected to the Internet. This chapter outlines your options, then explains how to obtain, install, configure and run Internet Explorer.

Covers

Introduction to the Internet

 HANDY TIP

This book is in three sections. Chapters 1–4 cover the things you need to know to start making use of Internet Explorer. Chapters 5–9 cover more advanced features, including the new Active Channels and Active Desktop. Chapters 10–13 introduce the additional applications supplied with the full version of Internet Explorer.

The Internet is a 'network of networks' which connects millions of computers from all around the world. It's estimated that over 50 million people use the Internet, and the number increases every day.

You can use the Internet to access the latest news; research almost any topic you can imagine; shop for products and services; or get information about your favourite sport, hobby, television programme, band or movie star. You can also send messages, participate in discussion groups and obtain software for your computer.

History of the Internet

The Internet has its roots in 1969, when the US Government decided to connect some of its computers together so scientists and military agencies could communicate more easily. The system was designed to be very robust, so there was no central control centre. Each machine operated independently and messages travelled by whichever route seemed most convenient at the time.

In the 1970s several more computer networks were established by military and academic institutions. Eventually many of these networks were linked together, creating the network of networks we now know as 'the Internet'. During the 1980s the Internet was dominated by scientists, academics, computer experts and students, but the user-friendly software of the 1990s has encouraged a much wider range of people to make use of it.

Although some parts of the world are better represented than others, the Internet is becoming a truly global phenomenon. You can connect to a computer in Australia or New Zealand just as easily – and as cheaply – as to one just down the road.

No one owns or controls the Internet, although there are various organisations which endeavour to keep everything running smoothly. It can be creaky, cranky and intensely irritating, but for the most part it works remarkably well.

...contd

The World Wide Web

The World Wide Web is not the same thing as the Internet. The Internet is a network of computers. The Web is a 'service' which makes use of that network. Other services include e-mail (Chapter 10) and newsgroups (Chapter 11).

The recent surge of interest in the Internet is due to the World Wide Web. Developed in 1990 at CERN, the European Laboratory for Particle Physics, the Web consists of millions of magazine-style pages. Unlike pages in a printed magazine, however, they can include sound samples, animations, video clips and interactive elements as well as text and pictures.

Web pages are connected together by 'hypertext' links – electronic cross-references which enable you to jump from page to page by clicking on underlined text or highlighted images. A page stored on a computer in London might have links to pages stored in Moscow, Tokyo and Washington, which in turn might be linked to pages in many other countries. The result is a network of connections stretching right around the globe – hence 'World Wide Web'.

You don't need to know where any of the pages are, because you can follow the links from one to the next. However, if you do know the address of the page you want to view, you can jump straight to it.

Turn to Chapter 4 for more information about a selection of the most popular pages on the Web.

Anyone can create a Web page, so there's a huge range of material to explore. Government departments, museums, educational institutions and charities are pouring information on to the Web, and many companies use it to promote their products or provide after-sales service. Publishers and broadcasters produce on-line magazines and news services, and you'll find many pages dedicated to the hobbies and interests of private individuals.

Web browsers

In order to look at – or 'browse' – Web pages, you need a piece of software called a 'Web browser'. It enables you to find Web pages and display them on your screen.

Internet Explorer is Microsoft's Web browser. It's popular, easy to use and free, so it's a good choice for beginners.

Connecting to the Internet

Before you can access the Web, you need to be connected to the Internet. There are three possibilities: your company or university may provide a direct connection; you can visit a cyber café or public library; or you can use a modem (a device which enables computers to communicate with each other over a phone line) to connect your home computer to the Internet.

Company connections

The rest of this chapter assumes you're using a dial-up connection (see opposite). If you are connecting from a university or company, ask your systems manager to help you install and configure Internet Explorer.

If you are at university, or work for a large company which has an internal computer network, you may already be connected to the Internet. Ask your systems manager if it's possible for you to access the World Wide Web from your PC, Macintosh or workstation.

The advantage of a company connection is that you don't have to pay for it. There are several disadvantages: you have to be at work to access the Internet; there may be rules about what you can use it for; and you have no control over the speed of the connection, which can be anything from excellent to awful.

Cyber cafés, pubs and libraries

The cyber café is the Internet equivalent of the public telephone, but is generally warmer and more comfortable. You can drink coffee (or beer, in a cyber pub) and use the café's computers to explore the Internet. Most charge by the half hour or hour, and the rates are quite reasonable. Your local library may also have computers you can use.

If you aren't sure whether the Internet is for you, paying to use someone else's equipment for a few hours is a good way to find out. You don't have to worry about setting up the software, and there's usually someone to help with any problems. You are, however, stuck with the programs which are provided, and you may not have access to the full range of Internet services – for example, you may not be able to send and receive e-mail.

Dial-up connections

The most versatile option is to use a modem to connect your own computer to the Internet. Regrettably, this is also the option which requires the most input – both financial and technical – from you.

You need five things to establish a dial-up connection:

1   A computer. Internet Explorer is available for PCs, Apple Macintoshes and Unix workstations, but this book concentrates on the version for PCs running Windows 95 or 98. You will need at least a 66MHz 486 with 8Mb of RAM (16Mb if you plan to install the Windows Desktop Update – see Chapter 9) and 60–100Mb of free hard disk space to use the Windows 95 version.

2   A modem. Modems come in two flavours – internal and external – and a range of speeds. It's a false economy to buy anything less than a 33,600bps (bits per second) modem; a slower modem may be cheaper, but you'll run up bigger phone bills.

3   A telephone line. If your phone company offers cheap deals on local calls, so much the better.

4   An Internet service provider (see page 12). A service provider has a computer system which is permanently connected to the Internet, and to a bank of modems. You use your modem to connect to one of the service provider's modems, via your telephone line, thereby making your computer (temporarily) part of the Internet.

5   Connection software (see page 14). You'll need a program to establish the connection.

Internet service providers

Service providers enable you to connect to the Internet via a modem and telephone line. Most also provide basic software and help you set it up. There are two types: regular service providers and on-line services.

Unless your telephone line is supplied by a company which offers free local calls, you'll also be running up your phone bill while you're connected to the Internet.

Regular service providers, such as BT Internet, Demon, Direct Connection and UUNET, simply provide your connection. They generally charge a flat monthly fee, no matter how much (or how little) time you spend on-line. You may also be charged a one-off start-up fee which covers the cost of setting up the account and supplying you with some Internet software.

On-line services, such as AOL, CompuServe, Line One and the Microsoft Network (MSN) provide extra facilities for their members, such as subscriber-only content and private discussion forums. Each service has its own software, which often includes a customised version of Internet Explorer.

On-line services usually have lower monthly fees than regular service providers, but the basic payment only entitles you to 3–5 hours on-line. Once you've used up your monthly allotment, you're charged by the hour. This means on-line services can be more expensive than regular service providers if you spend a lot of time on-line. However, they are an economic option if you stay within the monthly allotment, and some also offer flat-rate pricing schemes for people who want to make more intensive use of the Internet.

Most on-line services, and some regular service providers, offer one-month free trials for new users. Signing up for one of these trials is a good way to find out what you'll get for your money. As well as trying out the software, you can explore the member-only services and decide whether you're getting a good deal. If you decide not to continue, remember to ring up and close your account. If you don't, you'll be liable for the monthly charges.

Most Internet magazines publish up-to-date lists of Internet service providers. The things to consider when choosing a provider are:

1 Level of service. Make sure you'll be getting full Internet access, including e-mail, newsgroups and the Web. Find out what software is supplied, and whether you can use something else if you don't like it. If you're planning to create your own Web pages (see Chapter 13), ask about free Web space.

2 Points of Presence (PoPs). Find a service provider which has an access point within your local call area or uses a special number which is charged at the local-call rate, no matter where you call from.

3 Modem speed. Make sure your service provider supports the fastest speed your modem can manage.

4 Subscriber-to-modem ratio. If you choose a service provider which has a lot more subscribers than modems, you'll find it hard to get through. Aim for a ratio of around 15 subscribers per modem (15:1).

5 Technical support. Sooner or later you'll need to call your service provider's helpline. Find out how much the calls cost, and check the opening hours – a helpline which is only available during the day won't be much good if you're expecting to use the Internet after work or at the weekend. If you don't have much experience with computers, call up and ask a few questions. If the service provider you're considering can't answer them clearly, try someone else.

Connection software

You need special software to access the Internet – an ordinary comms package won't do.

These days, getting on the Internet usually just involves installing your service provider's software pack. You don't actually need to understand how the connection software works, but here's a quick guide for the curious.

Establishing a connection

Before you can run Internet Explorer, or any other Internet application, you need to persuade your modem to connect your computer to the Internet. You do this by running a small program called a 'winsock' (and sometimes described as a 'dialler'), which controls your modem.

The winsock not only handles the connection, but also establishes a TCP/IP interface, enabling other programs to send and receive data. TCP/IP stands for Transmission Control Protocol/Internet Protocol, and it's the common language of the Internet.

How the Internet works

Every computer on the Internet has a unique address, or 'IP number', which looks something like 194.88.75.43. The more important ones also have names, such as www.computerstep.com. The Domain Name System (DNS) converts the easy-to-remember names into computer-friendly numbers when you type in an address.

TCP and IP are responsible for getting data from one address to another. TCP breaks it up into small 'packets' and adds the address, then IP gets the packets to their destination, using any available route. At the other end, TCP checks that all the packets have arrived and reassembles them in the correct order.

If there's a problem somewhere along the way, the packets are automatically rerouted to avoid it. They might not all take the same route, and some packets might go missing and have to be re-sent, but everything should get there in the end – without any help from you. What you will notice is that packets don't always arrive in a steady stream. Because they travel independently, you tend to get a bunch of packets, and then a gap, and then another bunch, and so on.

Installing and using a winsock

There are two ways to acquire a winsock: you either get one as part of your start-up package, or you can set up the winsock built in to Windows.

1   If you've just signed up with an Internet service provider (see page 12), you should have received a basic software package. Follow the installation instructions and you'll end up with (among other things) a working winsock. You may not be told exactly what has been installed, because most providers like to keep the technical bits in the background, but if you can connect to the Internet and run the other programs in the package, you're in business.

2   If you didn't receive any software, don't like what you've been given or have an old account which you now want to set up under Windows 95/98, you'll need to set up the built-in winsock. Internet Explorer includes a Connection Wizard (see page 20) to help you do this.

Once the winsock has been installed and configured, you can use it to connect to your service provider's computer, or 'log on'. You then leave the winsock program running in the background while you use Internet Explorer.

When you've finished browsing the Web, you end your session by clicking the Disconnect button. This tells your modem to hang up, releasing the phone line for other calls. Most setups will drop the line if the modem is inactive for several minutes, but it's better to hang up straight away. There's no point paying for a connection you aren't using.

Obtaining Internet Explorer

Many service providers include a copy of Internet Explorer in their start-up package. Some high-street stores sell a boxed version, and you'll often find it on the CD-ROMs attached to the front of computer magazines. If you've only just bought your PC, you'll probably find that Internet Explorer has been pre-installed.

'Download' means to copy a file from a computer on the Internet to your computer. Uploading a file copies it from your computer to one on the Internet.

If you're already an Internet user, you can download Internet Explorer from Microsoft's Web site. You'll need plenty of patience, though – the Standard version takes a couple of hours to download.

1 Connect to Microsoft's Web site at:

`http://www.microsoft.com/ie/`

2 This page changes regularly, but it's always linked to the download area. Look for an Internet Explorer button

( ) or some underlined text which says 'Download'. Click the button or the text to move to the download pages.

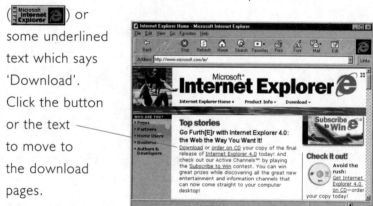

3 The download pages also change regularly. Read the instructions, then click the Download button.

4 Select the correct language (US English).

...contd

5 You will be presented with a list of locations from which you can download the setup program. Choose one which is close to home.

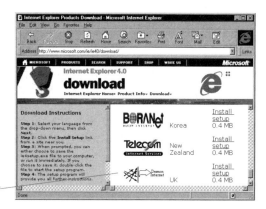

6 The setup program runs through the first part of the installation routine (see overleaf) to determine which files need to be downloaded. You can download and install the program in one operation, or simply download the files so you can install Internet Explorer later.

In addition to the Standard and Full installations, this version of the setup program gives you a Browser-only option which requires fewer files, thereby reducing the download time.

7 Once you've decided which components you want to install (see steps 2 to 4, overleaf), the setup program prompts you to choose a download site. It then fetches all the files.

8 If you selected the Install option in step 6, the setup program continues with the installation; otherwise you need to restart it when you're ready to install the software.

Installing Internet Explorer

If you're installing Internet Explorer from a disk supplied by your service provider, follow whatever instructions have been provided. They should include details of any service-specific settings or options. Likewise, if you've bought the boxed version, follow the on-screen instructions.

If you're installing Internet Explorer from a magazine's cover-mounted CD-ROM, you probably just have to pick the right menu option to start the setup program.

1 The Active Setup Wizard helps you install Internet Explorer.

2 Decide whether you want the Standard installation, which enables you to browse the Web, send e-mail and access newsgroups (see Chapters 10 and 11), or the Full installation, which also enables you to converse with other Internet users and design Web pages (Chapters 12 and 13).

3 The Windows Desktop Update makes a number of changes to the Windows 95 operating system, creating a more Internet-oriented environment (see Chapter 9). However, you can browse the Web perfectly well without it, and it's easy to add it later, so don't feel you have to install it now.

4 Select United Kingdom to install a selection of Channels (see Chapter 8) designed by local organisations such as the BBC, Sky, *New Scientist* and the *Financial Times.*

5 The Wizard then installs all the components you selected in steps 2 to 4.

6 Once the installation is complete, the Welcome screen appears. Click Start to tour the main features and find out about Channels.

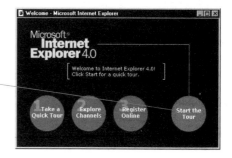

7 When you reach the Registration section, the program will determine whether your computer is set up to access the Internet. If it isn't, it will run the Internet Connection Wizard (see overleaf) to help you set up your account; otherwise it connects you to Microsoft's Web site so you can register your copy of Internet Explorer.

Setting up your connection

If your copy of Internet Explorer was supplied as part of a service provider's start-up package, the connection has probably been set up for you. If you've managed to connect to the Internet and register your software, skip to page 23.

If you need to configure the connection software yourself, the Internet Connection Wizard will appear when you try to register Internet Explorer. You'll need the following information to answer its questions:

1 The phone number you use to connect to the Internet.

2 Your user name and password.

3 Your e-mail address.

4 Names of your service provider's incoming (probably POP3, possibly IMAP) and outgoing (SMTP) mail servers.

5 User name and password for your mail account (probably the same as your regular user name and password).

6 Name of your service provider's news (NNTP) server.

7 User name and password for the news server (if required).

All this information should have been sent to you when you opened your account. If there's anything you can't find, give your service provider a ring.

Depending on your setup, you may also need your Windows installation disk.

...contd

These instructions should work for most people with standard dial-up accounts. If you have problems, you may need to go into the Advanced Settings section and enter some more information. Contact your service provider for advice.

Once you've collected all the information listed on the previous page, you can use the Internet Connection Wizard to set up your account.

1   There are three setup options. The first is for people who don't yet have Internet accounts. It connects you to Microsoft's Internet Referral Server so that you can choose a local service provider. Choose the second option if you've opened an account, but haven't started using it yet, or the third if your computer is already set up for Internet access. The rest of these instructions are for people who've chosen the second setup option.

2   Select 'Connect using my phone line'. Enter the number you call to connect to your service provider, then enter your user name and password.

3   The default settings should work for most people, so try clicking No on this screen. You can change the Advanced Settings later if there's a problem (see page 24).

4   Enter a name for the connection. The name of your service provider will do.

5 You are prompted to enter details of your e-mail account. If you haven't been given a separate e-mail user name and password, enter the ones you used in step 2.

6 Enter the name of your service provider's news server (used for Usenet newsgroups – see Chapter 11).

7 Unless you have an LDAP account, select 'No' to skip the Internet Directory Service section.

8 Click Finish to complete the setup process.

9 Restart your computer, then go to the Start menu and select Programs>Accessories>Dial-Up Networking. You should see an icon for your Internet account.

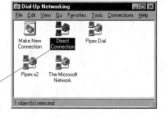

10 Double-clicking on the icon enables you to connect to your service provider's computer. You won't normally need to do this, though, because Internet Explorer activates the connection program automatically – see opposite.

Running Internet Explorer

To run Internet Explorer, double-click on its icon or select it from the Programs>Internet Explorer section of your Start menu. It should run your connection software automatically.

Internet Explorer

If you select 'Connect automatically', you won't need to click the Connect button in future.

1 Click Connect to dial into your service provider's computer and establish a connection.

2 Once your user name and password have been verified, the Internet Explorer window appears and you are taken to Microsoft's Web site. Chapter 2 explains how to move about this site and visit other places on the Web.

If your service provider has its own connection software, the procedures for connecting and disconnecting may be different.

3 If there are no other Internet programs running when you close Internet Explorer, you will be prompted to disconnect from the Internet. You can also disconnect by switching to the connection program and clicking the Disconnect button.

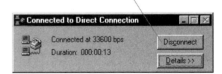

Fine-tuning your connection

You can alter the connection settings if you change service providers, or fine-tune them to suit your way of working.

| To change your settings, select Internet Options from Internet Explorer's View menu. Click the Connection tab.

You can also run the Wizard from the Start menu. Select Programs>Internet Explorer>Connection Wizard.

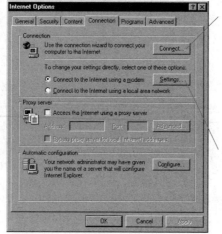

2 Click Connect to run the Internet Connection Wizard so you can set up a new account or change the details of your current one.

3 Click Settings to determine how Internet Explorer makes and breaks connections.

4 If you have several accounts, select the one which Internet Explorer should use.

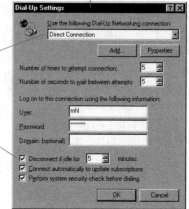

5 Specify how long the modem can remain idle before Internet Explorer drops the connection to avoid running up excessive bills (you get a 30-second warning).

6 Select 'Connect automatically...' to enable Internet Explorer to update Subscriptions while you're away from your computer (see Chapter 8).

Basic Web browsing

Chapter Two

Internet Explorer enables you to locate and view Web pages. This chapter shows you how to enter addresses and jump from page to page. It also explains what to do when you encounter images, sounds, video clips and program files. Finally, you'll learn how save and print Web pages.

Covers

Introducing Internet Explorer

Like most Windows programs, Internet Explorer has title, menu and tool bars across the top of the window, and a status bar at the bottom. The most important areas of the screen are:

Title bar –
displays the
name of
the page

Menu
bar

Standard
buttons

Address bar –
displays the address,
or URL, of the page

 Service providers can customise Internet Explorer, so your version may look slightly different.

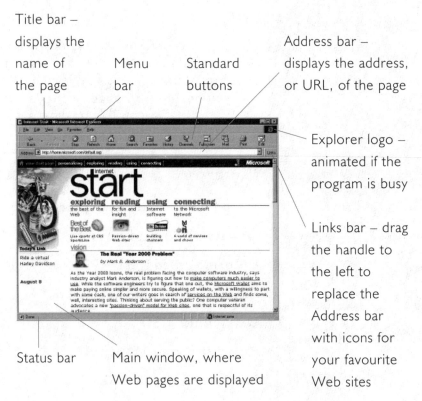

Explorer logo –
animated if the
program is busy

Links bar – drag
the handle to
the left to
replace the
Address bar
with icons for
your favourite
Web sites

Status bar

Main window, where
Web pages are displayed

 You can also increase the screen area by clicking the Fullscreen button or selecting View> Full Screen.

The Standard buttons, Address bar and Links bar are all part of the Toolbar. You can rearrange the sections or turn some of them off to increase the size of the main window.

1 To move a section of the Toolbar, use the mouse to grab the handle at the left-hand end. Drag it up, down or across.

2 To turn off a section of the Toolbar, go to View>Toolbar and deselect it. You can also shrink the Standard buttons by turning off their text labels.

Understanding addresses

Every page on the Web has a unique address. These addresses are called Uniform Resource Locators, or URLs. You've probably seen some in newspapers and magazines and on television.

 A page is a single Web document. Some are quite long – use the scroll bar to move through them. A site is a collection of related pages, and the server is the computer on which all the documents are stored.

The URL for the features section of Microsoft's Small Business Resource is:

`http://www.microsoft.com/smallbiz/feature.htm`

The 'http:' indicates that this is a Web page.

This is the name of the server where the page is stored.

This section tells your browser which folder the page is stored in.

This is the name of the document which describes the page.

Unless you tell it otherwise, Internet Explorer assumes you are looking for a Web page, so you don't have to type the `http://` at the beginning. If you're looking for the main page of a company's site, you can also leave out everything after the first single slash. To locate the main page of Microsoft's Web site, for example, you would enter: `www.microsoft.com`

Other addresses

You will also see URLs for other types of Internet site:

URL begins	Type of site
`ftp:`	FTP (see page 90)
`gopher:`	gopher (see page 91)
`mailto:`	e-mail address (see page 143)
`news:`	Usenet newsgroup (see page 158)

Entering an address

If you know the address of the Web page you wish to visit, you simply enter it into Internet Explorer. There are three ways to do this:

HANDY TIP

If Internet Explorer recognises the first part of the address, it will complete it automatically. Just press Enter to visit the page.

1 Type the address into the Address bar, then press the Enter key. Internet Explorer will find and display the page.

2 To re-enter an address which you have typed recently, click the arrow at the end of the Address bar and select it from the drop-down list.

HANDY TIP

Chapter 4 contains a selection of URLs for you to try.

3 If you have turned off the Toolbar, you can enter addresses by selecting Open from the File menu or pressing Ctrl+O.

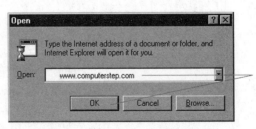

Both actions bring up the Open dialogue box. Enter the address and click the OK button.

Problems you may have

The Internet is constantly evolving: sites come and go and servers are constantly being moved or upgraded. It's also subject to its fair share of bugs and bad connections, so sometimes Internet Explorer will give you an error message instead of displaying the page you were looking for.

Three of the most common error messages are:

HANDY TIP

You can sometimes find a page which has moved by entering part of the URL. Start by leaving out everything after the last slash (/). If that doesn't work, keep chopping off sections until you get back to the name of the server (see page 27).

1 Not found. There are numerous variations on this message, but they all amount to one of two things: either you typed the URL incorrectly, or the page you are looking for has been moved or deleted.

HTTP/1.0 404 Object Not Found

The Internet Movie Database

Something wasn't found.

The URL you requested could not be found. The usual cause for this is an out of date link on another site.

Please try starting here instead.

2 Cannot open site. This usually occurs because the first part of the address is incorrect. Check your typing and try again.

3 Timed out. This message appears because the computer you are trying to connect to is busy or off-line. These problems often clear themselves quite quickly, so try again in a minute or two.

Using links

If you could only get to Web pages by typing in their URLs, browsing the Web would be tedious and time-consuming. Fortunately there's a much easier way to get about: links.

Almost every Web page is linked to anything from one to a hundred or more other pages. Links are usually indicated by coloured, underlined text, and you move to the linked page by clicking this text. For example:

REMEMBER

Links can also take you to another section of the same page. For example, many long pages have a list of the major subheadings at the top. Clicking on a heading takes you to the relevant section.

Here's a page from the Yahoo! Web directory (see page 56). If you click the blue underlined text which says 'Reference'...

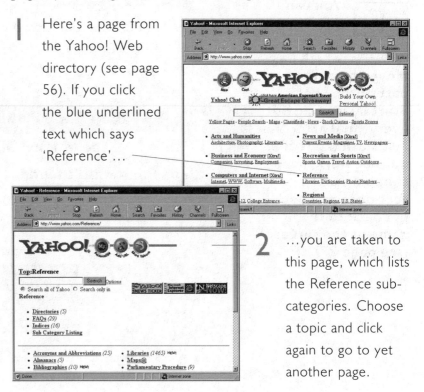

2 ...you are taken to this page, which lists the Reference sub-categories. Choose a topic and click again to go to yet another page.

You can tell when the mouse pointer is over a link, because it changes into a pointing hand ($\overset{\text{\tiny$\ast$}}{\text{\tiny $\circlearrowleft$}}$). While you're pointing, check the Status bar. You should see the name of the file or site at the other end of the link. The linked text usually changes colour after you've clicked it, so that you can see where you've been.

Images can also be used as links – see pages 34–5.

Retracing your steps

Browsing the Web is like exploring the back streets of an old market town – there are lots of directions to head in and it's easy to get lost. However, it's equally easy to retrace your steps.

1 To return to the page you just left, click the Back button, select Back from the Go menu or press Alt + Cursor Left.

You can use the History bar to return to any page you've visited in the last two or three weeks – see page 52.

2 To go back several pages, click the arrow to the right of the Back button. Select the page you want to revisit from the pop-up list.

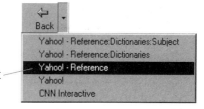

3 Once you've gone back a few pages, you may want to go forward again. Click the Forward button, select Forward from the Go menu or press Alt + Cursor Right. If you want to go forward several pages, click the arrow to the right of the Forward button.

4 If you get completely lost, you can start again by clicking the Home button or selecting Home Page from the Go menu. (The Home Page is the page Internet Explorer looks for each time you run it. It's usually a Microsoft page by default, but you can change it to anything you like – see page 48.)

Stop and Refresh

If the Internet is busy, Web pages can take a long time to arrive, so Internet Explorer enables you to end tedious downloads. You can then go somewhere else, or hope for a better connection and try again.

 The Internet Explorer logo () in the top right corner is animated when a page is downloading and becomes static when the transfer is complete. You can click on links as soon as you see the text, though – you don't have to wait for the rest of the page to arrive.

1 To abort a download, click the Stop button, select Stop from the View menu or press Esc. Internet Explorer gives up fetching the page.

2 If you change your mind and want to see the rest of a half-downloaded page, click the Refresh button, select Refresh from the View menu or press F5 to reload the page.

3 You can also use Refresh to make sure you're seeing the very latest version of a page. For example, pages showing sports results may be updated every few minutes, but the new data won't necessarily be sent to your computer. Sites which work this way usually instruct you to 'reload often'.

Understanding Web pages

Web pages start out as unformatted text files – the type of file your word processor produces when you save a file as 'text' or 'plain text'. The author then specifies how it should look by inserting pairs of 'tags'. To emphasise a phrase by displaying it in bold type, for example, they insert a 'bold on' tag at the beginning and a 'bold off' tag at the end. When you download the file, Internet Explorer reads the tags and adds the formatting.

HANDY TIP

To see what an HTML file 'really' looks like, open a Web page and select View>Source. Internet Explorer will transfer the file to Notepad, which displays the tags (look for things in angle <> brackets) as well as the text.

This system is known as HyperText Mark-up Language (HTML), and it's what makes the Web work. As well as enabling Web authors to format their pages, it makes it possible to include references to other files. Links, for example, are created using a pair of tags which say 'if someone clicks anywhere between here (link on) and here (link off), load file xyz'. It might not sound very exciting, but without the ability to include these instructions in the pages, the whole thing would fall apart. You'd have to know the location of every single page instead of just jumping from one to the next.

Tags can also be used to tell the browser to download additional files and insert them into the text. This is how the images arrive: Internet Explorer reads the HTML file, finds an instruction which tells it to 'insert image abc', fetches the image file, works out how everything should look and displays the page. This is why the text usually appears first: until you download the HTML file, Internet Explorer doesn't even know there should be pictures.

Unless you want to create your own Web pages (see Chapter 13), you don't need to worry about the ins and outs of HTML. However, you do need to remember that the pictures are stored separately from the text, as are sounds, video clips and other additional material.

There are lots of advantages to this 'bit by bit' approach. For example, you can tell Internet Explorer to ignore files which might take a long time to download (see overleaf). However, it does make it difficult to save a Web page on to your hard disk (see page 39).

Images

Images make the World Wide Web colourful and interesting, add personality and give it the 'friendly face' which modern computer users have become accustomed to. However, they are typically five to ten times larger than text files and take proportionately longer to download. If you're prepared to forgo aesthetics, you can speed things up tremendously by turning them off.

To turn off the images, select Internet Options from the View menu and click the Advanced tab. Scroll down to the Multimedia section and deselect Show pictures.

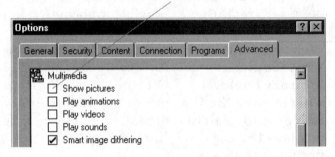

2   You'll probably want to deselect animations, videos and sounds at the same time.

The problem with turning off the images is that many of them aren't just there to decorate the page; they are also used as links. The most common types of image link are:

Buttons. Many Web sites use icons and toolbars to help you navigate. For example, the Yahoo! Web directory (see page 56) has buttons which take you to special sections of the site. Clicking the Yahoo! logo takes you to the main page.

2 Text. When Web page designers want to use a special font, create fancy text effects or combine text with graphics, they have to save it as an image file. The result may not look like 'regular' linked text, but it functions the same way.

Gardening Basics

Backyard Builder

Landscaping

Instant Gardening

	Look up a plant	Check your weather
Talk to a gardener	Search VG	Locate your zone
Toolshed	Dig the Net	Find a source	VG At-a-glance

For example, Pathfinder's Virtual Garden site (see page 64) uses four small images to create the menu shown above, plus a larger one for the strip across the bottom.

3 Image maps. Some images contain more than one link. For example, this picture from the BBC's *Blue Peter* Web site (see page 70), is linked to Web pages for the four presenters. When you click a person, you're taken to their page. It's called an image map because different parts of the image are 'mapped' to different Web site addresses.

Stuart

You can find out whether an image is a link by moving the mouse pointer over it. If it changes to a pointing hand, just as it does over a text link (see page 30), clicking will take you to another page.

Sounds and videos

Sound samples and video clips can be embedded in a Web page, in which case they are downloaded and played automatically. (If you have a slow connection, you can tell Internet Explorer not to bother – see page 34.) However, it's more common for the files to be linked to the page, so you can decide whether you want to hear or view them.

Playing a linked sound or video is a two-step process: first you download the file, then you use the tape deck-style controls to play the clip.

1 To play a sound or video, such as this recording from NASA's Shuttle Web site (see page 78), click the link leading to the file.

Other Audios
Prelaunch Poll
(1.8mb)
Crew Wakeup Calls

REMEMBER **Internet Explorer supports most common audio formats, including Windows (wav), Macintosh (aiff) and basic audio (au and snd). You can also play Video for Windows (avi), QuickTime (qt and mov) and MPEG movies. If you encounter an exotic new format, you may need to install additional software – see Chapter 6.**

2 Select 'Open this file' to activate the player window. The blue line creeps across to the right, indicating the progress of the download.

3 Click the Play button to hear the sound or watch the video clip.

poll.wav at shuttle.nasa.gov

0 1:26
DOWNLOADING

00:00
TIME

62.57% of 1352K

You don't always have to wait for the file to finish downloading before you start playing the clip. Check the Play button – if it's active (rather than greyed out), you can play the first few seconds as soon as the blue line has moved a few millimetres across the screen. It's a good idea to do this with large files, in case the rest isn't worth the wait. Close the player window to abort the transfer.

Downloading program files

You can download lots of software from the Internet, including public domain and shareware programs, demo versions of commercial software and add-ons for many programs. Internet Explorer enables you to fetch and run these files in a single operation, but you'll almost always want to save them on to your hard disk instead. You can then experiment with your new software once you've disconnected from the Internet.

1   To download a program file, such as these sample games available from Microsoft's Web site (see page 54), click the appropriate link.

Rattler Race: a sample Entertainment Pack Game for Windows Eat apples and avoid bouncing balls and other snakes. (67 KB, published 1/02/96)

Rodent's Revenge: a sample Entertainment Pack Game for Windows Trap the Cats in a puzzle maze of your own doing. (60 KB, published 3/1/96)

There's always a chance that a downloaded program might contain a virus. See page 105 for more information.

2   Internet Explorer asks whether you want to open (run) the file or save it on to your hard disk. Choose 'Save this program to disk' and click OK.

3   The standard Save As dialogue box appears. Select a folder and click Save.

4   The file is then downloaded on to your hard disk – this often takes several minutes. You can continue browsing while it downloads, or switch to another application and carry on working.

5   The file ends up in the folder you specified. Once you've logged off, you can locate and run it.

Compressed files

Web page authors often use compression programs to 'archive' the program files linked to their pages. Creating an archive packs everything – setup utility, documentation, help files and the program itself – into a single neat package. The archive is usually substantially smaller than the original group of files, so it downloads more quickly.

You'll also come across self-extracting archives – these have an .exe extension and unzip themselves when you run them.

The most popular compression program on the PC, PKZIP, produces archives with a .zip extension. Follow the instructions on the previous page to save them on to your hard disk.

Once you have downloaded a .zip file, you'll need to decompress or 'unzip' it. There are numerous shareware unzippers, but PKZIP for Windows is the best choice for beginners. You can get a copy from PKWARE's Web site at: http://www.pkware.com/

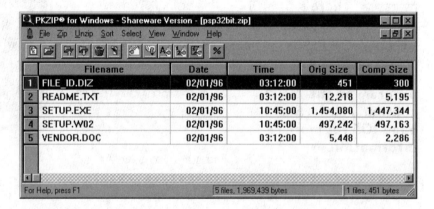

	Filename	Date	Time	Orig Size	Comp Size
1	FILE_ID.DIZ	02/01/96	03:12:00	451	300
2	README.TXT	02/01/96	03:12:00	12,218	5,195
3	SETUP.EXE	02/01/96	10:45:00	1,454,080	1,447,344
4	SETUP.W02	02/01/96	10:45:00	497,242	497,163
5	VENDOR.DOC	02/01/96	03:12:00	5,448	2,286

Other types of archive you may encounter include .hqx, .sit, .sea (Macintosh), .gz, .Z, .tar and .gtar (Unix) files. It's unlikely you'll be able to make use of the contents of these files, so it's best to avoid them.

Saving Web pages

Sometimes you'll want to read a lengthy Web page at your leisure, without worrying about your phone bill. You might also want to keep some information handy for reference. The easiest solution is to save the page on to your hard disk. You can then reload it whenever you want.

If you're only going to read a page once, there's no need to save it – just log off. The page will still be loaded and you can scroll through it as usual.

1 To save a Web page, pull down the File menu and select Save As. This brings up the standard Windows Save As dialogue box.

2 Choose a folder and give the file a name, then click Save. This only saves the text. If you want the images as well, you have to save them separately – see below.

3 To reload a saved page, select Open from the same menu, or press Ctrl+O. Click the Browse button, locate the file and click Open.

Don't forget that material on the Web is protected by copyright. Keeping copies for personal reference is unlikely to get you into trouble, but you mustn't reuse or redistribute text, images, sounds or videos without the owner's permission.

You can also save images, sounds and videos.

1 To save an image, right-click it and select Save Picture As from the pop-up menu. If you want to display it on your desktop, select Set As Wallpaper instead.

2 To save a sound or video, such as this NASA clip (see page 78), right-click in the player window and select Save As.

Printing Web pages

If you're gathering information for a report or project, printing Web pages is sometimes more convenient than saving them. Printing a page preserves the images as well as the text, without filling up your hard disk, and you can scribble notes in the margins or highlight important passages. You can also print a table showing all the Web pages linked to the current one.

HANDY TIP

You can also print a page by clicking the Print button, but you'll bypass the Print dialogue and won't be able to change any of the options.

1 To print the current page, pull down the File menu and select Print, or press Ctrl+P.

2 If the page has frames (see page 84), you need to specify how they should be handled.

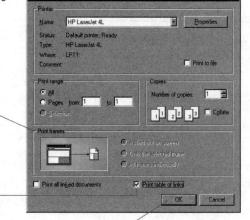

3 To include details of any linked Web pages, select 'Print table of links'.

4 Click the OK button to print the page.

Finding your way

There are over 50 million Web pages and it's easy to lose your way as you jump from one to the next. This chapter explains how to use Favorites, Shortcuts and the Links bar to keep track of the ones you visit regularly. It also shows you how to find information on the Web.

Covers

Chapter Three

Creating Favorites

As you explore the Web, you'll often come across sites which you may want to visit again in the future. Rather than writing down the address, you can add the site to Internet Explorer's Favorites menu. This menu is like the Programs section of the Start menu, except that selecting an item takes you to a Web site rather than running a program.

 HANDY TIP **You can also create Favorites by right-clicking on the page. Right-clicking on a link creates a Favorite for the page at the other end.**

To create a Favorite for the current page, select Add to Favorites from the Favorites menu.

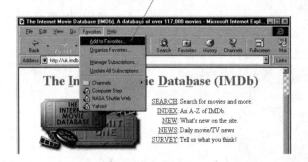

 HANDY TIP **Subscribing to Web sites is covered in Chapter 8.**

2 Select 'No, just add the page...' You may also want to change the default name to something shorter or clearer. Once you've done so, click OK.

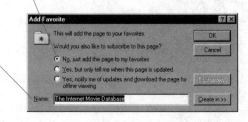

 HANDY TIP **See page 65 to find out more about the Internet Movie Database.**

3 You can now return to this page any time you want, simply by selecting it from the Favorites menu.

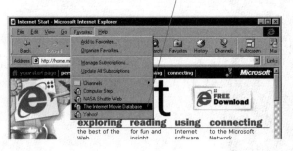

Managing Favorites

Once you have 15–20 Favorites, you'll need to start organising them into folders. This creates submenus and makes it easier to find the one you want.

1 Select Organize Favorites from the Favorites menu.

2 Click the Create New Folder ( ) button, then type in a name for your folder and press Enter.

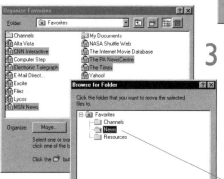

3 Select all the Favorites which should go into a particular folder (hold down Shift or Ctrl to select more than one at once). Click Move, select the folder and click OK.

4 Click Close to finish organising your Favorites.

HANDY TIP

To save a new Favorite into the correct folder, click the Create in>> button (see step 2, opposite) before you click OK.

5 Your Favorites menu now has submenus. To access them, hold the mouse pointer over the folder's menu entry until the submenu appears.

6 You can also use the Organize Favorites dialogue to rename or delete Favorites.

Favorites bar

The new Favorites bar provides another way to access your Favorites. It's more convenient than the menu, but takes up a quite a lot of the main window.

1 Click the Favorites button to open the Favorites bar.

HANDY TIP

If you switch to Full-screen mode (see page 26), the Favorites bar slides in and out from the left-hand side of the screen, enabling you to access the list of sites *and* use all of the main window.

2 Click a folder to see a list of Favorites. A second click closes the folder.

3 Click a Favorite to open a Web page (in this case CNN's – see page 62), in the main window.

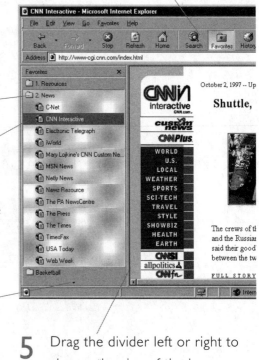

4 Click the arrows at the top and bottom to scroll through the list.

5 Drag the divider left or right to change the size of the bar.

6 Click the Favorites button again to close the Favorites bar. Alternatively, click the cross (**X**) in the top right corner of the bar.

...contd

You can also use the Favorites bar to reorganise your Favorites. It not only enables you to move, delete and rename both Favorites and folders, but also makes it possible to change their order.

1 To find out the address of one of your favourite sites, hold the mouse over it until a yellow label appears.

2 To delete or rename a folder or Favorite, right-click on it and select the appropriate option from the pop-up menu.

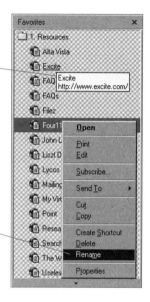

HANDY TIP

Favorites are normally displayed alphabetically. You can override this by dragging them into some other order.

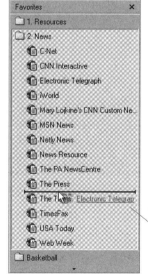

3 To move a folder or Favourite, point to it with the mouse, then press and hold the left button.

4 Drag the selected item to a new location. You can move it to a particular position in the list by looking out for the black divider which appears when the mouse pointer is between two items.

Internet Shortcuts

An Internet Shortcut is a Favorite which lives on your Desktop, rather than in the Favorites menu. Double-clicking on it connects you to the Internet, runs Internet Explorer and takes you to the specified page.

Internet Shortcuts are useful if there are a handful of sites which you visit regularly. For example, you might use a Shortcut to a news site, such as CNN Interactive (see page 62), to start Internet Explorer in the morning. Later in the day you might want to use a search engine or go straight to a sports or entertainment site.

1 To create an Internet Shortcut, right-click on the background of the Web page and select Create Shortcut from the pop-up menu. Alternatively, go to the File menu and select Send>Shortcut To Desktop.

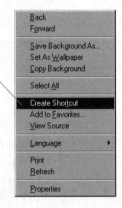

2 A dialogue box appears. Click OK to confirm the creation of the Shortcut.

3 The Shortcut is placed on your desktop. Double-click on it to start Internet Explorer and load the specified page (if Internet Explorer is already running, double-clicking on a Shortcut simply takes you to the page).

CNN
Interactive

Links bar

The Links bar provides yet another way to access your favourite sites. When you install Internet Explorer, it usually contains buttons for five Microsoft sites, but you don't have to stick with this selection. You can supplement Microsoft's choices with your own top sites.

1 Move the Links bar into a convenient position by dragging the handle at its left-hand end.

2 If you don't find the default links useful, drag them to the Windows Recycle Bin. Alternatively, right-click on them and select Delete from the pop-up menu.

There are several ways to create new buttons.

3 To add the current page, go to Favorites>Add to Favorites, then click Create in>> and select the Links folder.

4 Another option is to open the Favorites bar and drag a few of your Favorites on to the Links bar. You need to place them alongside the existing buttons – a black divider appears when the mouse is in the right place.

5 You can also select any link on a Web page and add the corresponding site to the Links bar. Point to the link, hold down the right mouse button and drag it on to the bar.

6 If you add more Links than Internet Explorer can display, arrows appear at both ends of the Links bar so you can scroll backwards and forwards.

Home page

The term 'home page' has several meanings. It can also refer to a personal Web page or the main page of a Web site.

The Home page is the page Internet Explorer looks for each time you run it. You're also taken to this page when you click the Home button or select Home Page from the Go menu.

The default Home Page is usually the Internet Start Page on Microsoft's Web site, although you may be taken to one of your service provider's pages instead. You don't have to stick with the default settings, though – you can change the Home page to any page you visit often or find useful, such as a news site or Web directory.

If you know the URL, you can just type it into the Address box.

1   To change your Home page, browse to the site you'd like to use. Select Internet Options from the View menu and click the General tab.

2   Click Use Current to change your Home page.

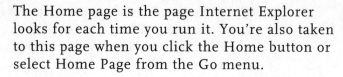

3   Click Use Default to revert to the default Home page.

4   Click Use Blank if you often want to run Internet Explorer without connecting to the Internet. It will load a blank page from your hard disk instead of running the connection software.

Searching the Internet

Browsing aimlessly round the Internet is easy – you just keep clicking links until you come across something interesting. More often than not, though, you'll be looking for specific information. If you were in a library, you'd consult the catalogue; on the Internet you turn to the organisations and individuals who devote their time to indexing the World Wide Web.

There are three basic types of index. Directories list sites by topic and subtopic, enabling you to focus in on the area of interest gradually. If you are looking for an explanation of Albert Einstein's Theory of Relativity, for example, you select Science, and then Physics, Relativity and so on. Web directories work well when you're researching a broad area.

In addition to search engines which cover the entire Web, you'll also encounter more specialised ones which concentrate on particular topics or sites. The technology is the same; they just use a smaller database.

If you're looking for something more specific, you're better off using a search engine. Search engines enable you to search or 'query' a vast database which indexes all the text on millions of Web pages. You simply type in a few keywords – Albert, Einstein and relativity, perhaps – and the site returns a list of all the Web pages where they appear. In most cases you also get a brief extract which helps you work out which pages are relevant.

Search engines are thorough but not very bright. They'll often return thousands or tens of thousands of 'hits', all of which contain your keywords, but few of which answer your question. If you choose your keywords carefully, though (see page 51), they can be very efficient.

The third type of index is a meta-list – a page of links dedicated to a particular subject, sometimes with brief descriptions of each site. Meta-lists are usually prepared by people who've spent a lot of time tracking down useful sites and want to share the results.

A search may take you through all three types of index. A Web directory might point you to a meta-list, which might recommend a site, which in turn might have a search engine which helps you find the most relevant page.

Search bar

Internet Explorer's Search bar provides easy access to a number of popular directories and search engines. It displays the Search dialogue down the left-hand side of the screen, enabling you to keep the results in view while you check out individual sites in the main window.

1 Click the Search button to open the Search bar.

2 Enter your keywords.

3 Select a search engine and click the Search button.

HANDY TIP

You can use the Address bar to search Yahoo! (see page 56). Type 'go', followed by the word or words you want to find, and press Enter.

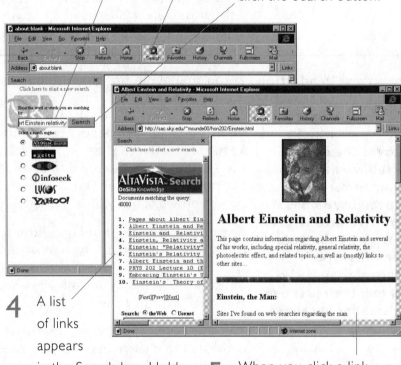

HANDY TIP

Studying physics? The site shown here can be found at:
`http://sac.uky.edu/~msunde00/hon202/Einstein.html`

4 A list of links appears in the Search bar. Hold the mouse over the titles for more information.

5 When you click a link, the corresponding page appears on the right.

The Search bar is very convenient, but it doesn't tell you how to make the most of the various services. It's a good idea to visit their home pages (see pages 56–8 for some addresses) to find out about any special facilities they offer.

Searching tips

Searching the Internet can be frustrating, but with practice it's possible to locate information quickly and efficiently.

1   Decide whether you're searching or browsing. If you're looking for general information about a broad topic, such as 'relativity', use a directory to find sites which concentrate on that subject. If you're looking for a specific person or event, use a search engine.

2   Visit the search engine's home page and read the instructions. The popular services all have slightly different options, and what works with one won't necessarily work with another. Once you've found an engine you like, stick with it – the others may find a slightly different selection of sites, but you won't miss much.

 HANDY TIP **If you're taken to a long page and can't work out where your keywords appear, select Edit> Find or press Ctrl+F to search the text.**

3   Think words, not concepts. Most search engines simply look for documents containing your keywords, so don't try to describe the concept – you'll get better results by thinking of terms which are likely to appear in the text.

4   Refine your search with phrases and extra terms. Most engines allow you to specify that two or more words should appear together, or that the documents must contain some words and not others. Searching for 'John' and 'Smith' finds over a million pages; searching for the phrase 'John Smith' brings it down to 9,000; and searching for 'John Smith' plus 'Labour' gives you around 100 hits, the majority of which deal with the late politician.

5   Use alternatives. Try 'movie' as well as 'film', and don't forget that 'football' is 'soccer' to many people.

History bar

If there's any chance you might want to return to a page, it's a good idea to make a Favorite or Shortcut for it, because deleting the ones you don't use is much easier than retracing your steps. However, all isn't lost if you haven't – you can use the History bar to return to any page you've visited in the last couple of weeks.

1 Click the History button to open the History bar.

2 Click the correct day, then find the server where the page resides.

See page 65 to find out more about the Internet Movie Database.

3 When you find the page you want to return to, click the title to load it into the main window.

You can specify how long the records should be kept. You might want to increase the storage period if you don't log on very often.

1 Go to View>Internet Options and click the General tab.

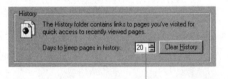

2 Use the up and down arrows to adjust the number of days the information remains in the History folder.

Exploring the Web

The Internet has so much to offer that it's hard to know where to start. The best way to learn about the Web is by exploring it, so here's a selection of useful, interesting and entertaining sites which provide a good introduction.

Chapter Four

Covers

Microsoft

**Microsoft
http://www.microsoft.com/**

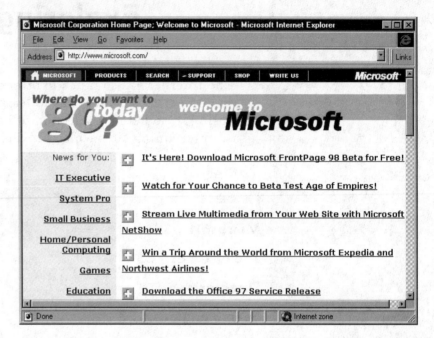

Microsoft's Internet Start Page (`http://home.microsoft.com/`) presents only a small sample of the software giant's on-line offerings. The main site has masses of information about the company's products, including Windows, Word, Excel, the many multimedia CD-ROMs and, of course, Internet Explorer. You can download demos and add-ons, or use the Support section to solve technical problems. The Knowledge Base – a huge database of solutions and step-by-step guides used by Microsoft's technical support staff – is worth a look if one of your applications is playing up.

The Internet

CNet
http://www.cnet.com/

CNet: The Computer Network is an American company which combines television programming and Web sites to provide information about computers, the Internet and future technology. The main site offers a beginner-friendly mixture of reviews, features and columns, including 'how to' guides, a glossary and a catalogue of Internet software. Other sites specialise in technology news, Web browsers, shareware and computer games.

You could also try:

HotWired, the electronic incarnation of *Wired* magazine. Iconoclastic but somewhat impenetrable, it sets trends as well as documenting them. Find it at:
http://www.hotwired.com/

For a UK perspective, try the on-line version of *.net* at:
http://www.netmag.co.uk/

Directories

Yahoo!
http://www.yahoo.com/

HANDY TIP

Most of the sites featured in this chapter are large, well established and unlikely to move or vanish. If you do find that one of the addresses is no longer valid, you may still be able to find the site using a directory or search engine.

Yahoo! is a hierarchical directory of Web sites and (some) other Internet resources. Each of the 14 categories is progressively subdivided into more tightly defined subcategories, enabling you to work your way down to a list of sites which concentrate on the subject of interest. It's extensively cross-referenced and you can speed things up by searching for keywords.

Yahoo! has several more specialised offshoots, including Yahooligans! for younger browsers, Yahoo! UK & Ireland and the customisable My Yahoo!

You could also try:

YELL, a UK Web directory brought to you by Yellow Pages. It isn't as comprehensive as Yahoo!, but it's useful if you're looking for UK sites. Find it at:
http://www.yell.co.uk/

Search engines

Alta Vista
http://www.altavista.digital.com/

Alta Vista enables you to search for Web sites and Usenet newsgroups containing a particular word or phrase. It takes some practice to get the best out of it – it's easy to make your search too broad, producing thousands of hits – but it does enable you to find information very quickly.

You could also try:

Lycos, which also indexes sounds, pictures, personal Web pages and sites deemed to fall within the top five per cent of all Web sites. Find it at:

http://www.lycos.com/

Excite, which enables you to refine your search by clicking the 'More like this' link next to an entry which hits the mark. If you opt for the UK version, you can restrict your search to UK or European sites. Find it at:

http://www.excite.co.uk/

Filez
http://www.filez.com/

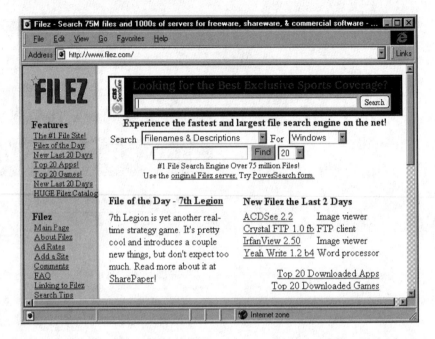

The Filez database has details of over 75,000 files stored on FTP sites (see page 90), enabling you to find programs, graphics, movies, sounds, icons and so on. You can search by name or, more usefully, description. It's also possible to specify a particular operating system (such as Windows) or type of file (such as graphics).

You could also try:

Four11, for e-mail addresses (see Chapter 10), at:
`http://www.four11.com/`

Deja News, which enables you to search Usenet newsgroups (see Chapter 11), at:
`http://www.dejanews.com/`

CNet's Search.com has links to over 100 specialist resources. Find it at:
`http://www.search.com/`

Best and worst

The Web 100
http://www.web100.com/

The Web 100 lists the best sites on the Web, as voted for by Internet users. The list is updated every hour, can be viewed by subject as well as ranking and includes a brief review of each site. Most of the voters are American, so some sites are too US-oriented to hold much interest for British Internet users. However, you'll also find plenty of must-see sites with international appeal.

You could also try:

Lycos, which reviews, rates and categorises the top five per cent of Web sites, at:
`http://point.lycos.com/categories/`

Cool Site of the Day, for a daily pointer to a Web site considered 'cool', at:
`http://cool.infi.net/`

The Useless Pages, for a selection of pointless sites, at:
`http://www.go2net.com/internet/useless/`

Service providers

InetUK
http://www.limitless.co.uk/inetuk/

InetUK maintains a list of service providers in the UK and Ireland, with links to their Web sites. It's handy if you're thinking of changing providers.

You could also try:

Your own service provider's Web site, which may provide technical support as well as details of its services. The information you were sent when you opened your account should include the address.

News and weather

The Electronic Telegraph
http://www.telegraph.co.uk/

The on-line edition of *The Telegraph* has everything you'd expect in a printed newspaper, including UK, international and City news, sport, weather, crossword, cartoons and classified ads. Catch up on older stories by searching the archive, which goes back to November 1994.

You could also try:

The Times, for on-line versions of both the daily and Sunday broadsheets. You can also combine your favourite sections to create a personal edition. Find it at:
`http://www.the-times.co.uk/`

The PA News Centre, for headline news from the Press Association's news agencies plus sports, television and radio schedules and weather forecasts. Find it at:
`http://www.pa.press.net/`

The Financial Times, for business news. Find it at:
`http://www.ft.com/`

CNN Interactive
http://www.cnn.com/

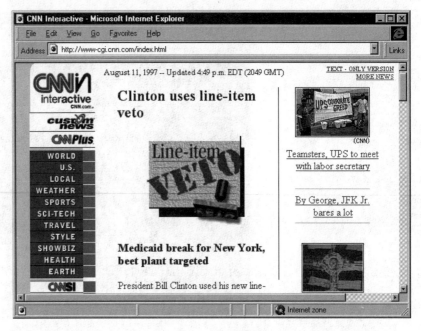

One of the great things about the Internet is the tremendous choice of viewpoints. Rather than sticking to British news sites, for example, you can pop over to the States for an American perspective on US and world news.

CNN's site provides a wide range of clearly presented stories, complete with sound samples and video clips. It's updated throughout the day and there are lots of cross-references and links to other sites. It also has message boards where you can comment on the news.

You could also try:

USA Today, the on-line version of the USA's biggest-selling general-interest paper. Find it at:
`http://www.usatoday.com/`

News Resource, for links to on-line news services from all around the globe, at:
`http://newo.com/news/`

The BBC Weather Centre
http://www.bbc.co.uk/weather/

Come rain or shine, the BBC Weather Centre brings you forecasts, weather lore and information about its services. You can meet the team and find out how the 54 daily broadcasts are made, or look up some of those mysterious meteorological terms. There's also a Daily Almanac which presents an 'on this day' collection of weather trivia.

You could also try:
The Met Office, for information about weather forecasting (but little in the way of forecasts), at:
`http://www.meto.govt.uk/`

Most UK news services (see page 61) publish forecasts.

Entertainment

Time Warner's Pathfinder
http://www.pathfinder.com/

Billed as "the Web's most complete news, information and entertainment site", the Pathfinder Network is an enormous complex of Time Warner sites. In addition to on-line versions of CNN (see page 62) and popular US magazines such as *Time, Life, Fortune, People* and *Entertainment Weekly,* it has an extensive lifestyle section. Highlights of the latter include the Virtual Garden and an upbeat health and fitness section called Thrive.

You could also try:

Warner Bros, for information about the company's movies, television shows, cartoons and comic books, at:
http://www.warnerbros.com/

Disney's Web site, which features everyone from Mickey Mouse to the heroes of *Toy Story*, at:
http://www.disney.com/

Movies

The Internet Movie Database
http://uk.imdb.com/

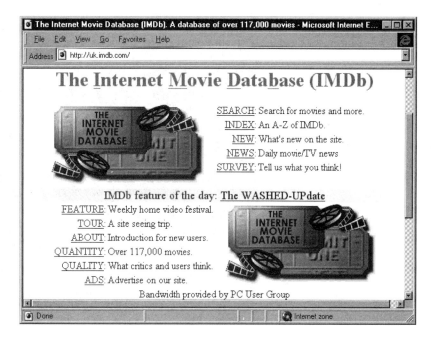

The Internet Movie Database contains everything you're likely to want to know about over 117,000 movies. As well as cast lists, synopses and reviews, it has links to everything from official studio sites to fan pages for directors and actors.

You could also try:

Mr Showbiz, an entertaining celebrity-oriented site which supplements its news and reviews with profiles, interviews, games and polls. Find it at:

`http://www.mrshowbiz.com/`

Most major releases have promotional Web sites with pictures, sound and video clips, games and so on. Use the Internet Movie Database to track them down.

YELL (see page 56) has a film-finding service with programme details for 450 UK cinemas.

Television

The BBC
http://www.bbc.co.uk/

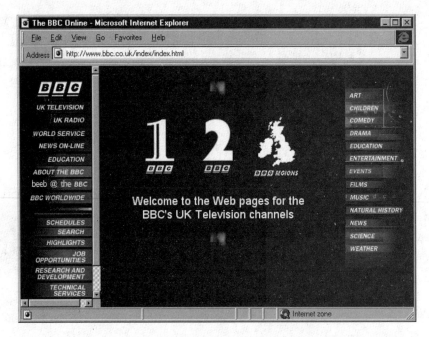

The BBC's Web site provides on-line support for a selection of television and radio programmes, including *Tomorrow's World, Watch Out, The Archers* and *Woman's Hour.* It's handy for looking up details you would have written down, if only you'd had a pen, and sometimes has additional material. You can also view schedules and highlights.

Beeb @ the BBC (http://www.beeb.com/) provides a home for *Radio Times, Top Gear,* the Comedy Zone and a sports magazine called *The Score!*

You could also try:

Channel 4, for listings, supplemental information and links to related sites, at:
http://www.channel4.com/

Yearling, for personalised TV listings covering 60 channels. Find it at:
http://www.yearling.com/

Music

MTV Online
http://www.mtv.com/

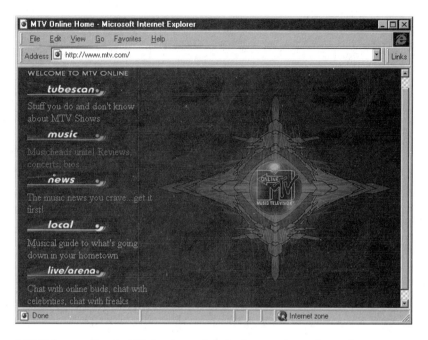

MTV has a lively Web site with information about its shows, music news, reviews and features, and lots of multimedia extras. If you're interested in a specific artist, label, event or publication, follow the links to UnfURLed (`http://www.unfurled.com/`), an MTV/Yahoo! (see page 56) guide to music sites elsewhere on the Web.

You could also try:
Jazz Online, an interactive publication specialising in all styles of jazz music, including mainstream, contemporary and acid. Find it at:
`http://www.jazzonln.com/`

Classical Insites, for information about composers, performers, recordings, genres and historical periods, at:
`http://www.classicalinsites.com/`

Magazines

Planet Science
http://www.newscientist.com/

Many popular magazines have Web sites which feature extracts and additional material.

The electronic incarnation of *New Scientist* mixes articles from the latest issue with Web-only supplements. You don't need to be a boffin to enjoy it, because it's written in layman's language and covers everyday science as well as leading-edge developments. It also has a database of jobs.

You could also try:

FutureNet, the on-line home of Future Publishing's stable of computing, entertainment and leisure titles, at:
`http://www.futurenet.com/`

The Electronic Newsstand has links to the on-line editions of over 2,000 magazines. Find it at:
`http://www.enews.com/`

E-zines

Salon
http://www.salonmagazine.com/

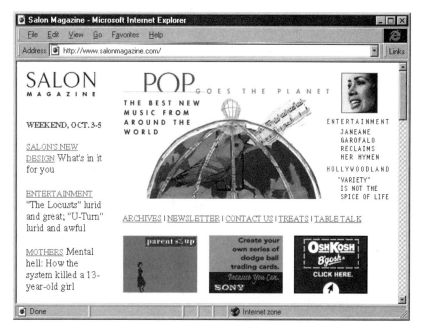

The ease and speed with which Web pages can be created has also spawned a host of Web-only magazines or 'e-zines'.

Salon is a literary e-zine covering "books, arts and ideas". In addition to Sunday supplement-style features, it has interviews, news and media commentary, reviews, travel, technology and taste sections and 'table talk' forums. It concentrates on quality writing and is updated daily.

You could also try:
Word, for high-tech cultural commentary, at:
http://www.word.com/

Women's Wire, for a female perspective on careers, money, style, entertainment and personal development, at:
http://www.women.com/

John Labowitz lists over 1,800 e-zines at:
http://www.meer.net/~johnl/e-zine-list/

Family

Blue Peter
http://www.bbc.co.uk/bluepeter/

The *Blue Peter* section of the BBC Web site (see page 66) enables children to meet the presenters – and their pets – and find out what happens behind the scenes. It also has contact details for organisations and activities featured on the programme. If you're stuck for something to do, the 'Here's one I made earlier' section is packed with recipes and things to make.

You could also try:

Children's Television Workshop, for games and stories featuring the Muppets from *Sesame Street*, at:
`http://www.ctw.org/`

The Kids section of the Warner Bros site, which has games, karaoke, a 'how we do it' guide to animation and other cartoon-related fun. Find it at:
`http://www.kids.warnerbros.com/`

Yahooligans! (see page 56) lists lots of good sites for kids.

Shopping

Bookpages
http://www.bookpages.co.uk/

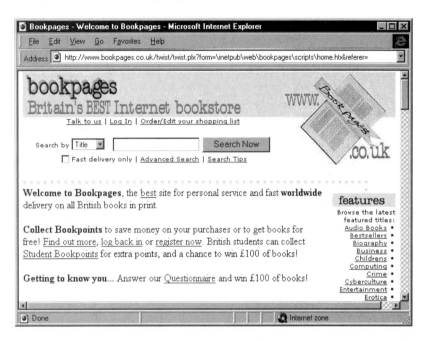

You should read the Privacy section of the Internet security chapter (page 108) before you use your credit card on-line.

Purchase books from the comfort of your keyboard by selecting from the 900,000-title database at Bookpages. It sells all the books currently in print in the United Kingdom and has reviews of selected titles.

You could also try:

The Internet Bookshop (iBS), for more of the same, at
`http://www.bookshop.co.uk/`

The Internet Music and Video Shop (iMVS) for over 150,000 music and video titles, at:
`http://www.musicshop.co.uk/`

Barclay Square, an on-line shopping mall, at:
`http://www.barclaysquare.co.uk/`

Sport and recreation

Lord's
http://lords.msn.com/

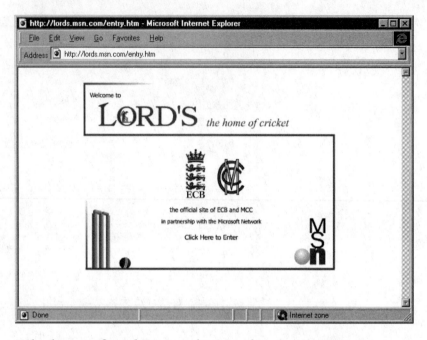

"The home of cricket" is split into three areas covering news, the current England team/tour and background information. Highlights include constantly updated scoreboards for First Class matches and live images from a camera on top of the Pavilion. There's also a fact file for each of the 18 First Class counties and an indexed and cross-referenced copy of the Official Laws of Cricket.

You could also try:

Soccernet, a *Daily Mail* co-production which comes in four flavours: English, Scottish, European and Global. The first two have news, results, league tables, match reports, gossip and lots of information about the top teams, while the others concentrate on news and tournaments. Find it at: http://www.soccernet.com/

NBA.com
http://www.nba.com/

Having access to the Internet makes it easy to follow sports which aren't popular in the UK, such as baseball, basketball and American football. You can also get up-to-the-minute results from international events.

The NBA site enhances its news, previews, results and profiles with lots of multimedia extras, including sound samples and videos. You can also e-mail questions to selected players or join on-line chat sessions. There are more statistics than you could shoot through a hoop and it's frighteningly thorough.

You could also try:
Fastball, for Major League baseball, at:
http://www.fastball.com/

NFL.com, for the (American) National Football League, at:
http://www.nfl.com/

Gorp
http://www.gorp.com/

The Great Outdoor Recreation Pages provide reams of information for people who prefer getting out and about to participating in (or watching) team sports. In addition to places to go and things to do (everything from biking and camping to hang-gliding and diving), the site covers books, trips, gear, eclectica (food, health, humour) and jobs.

You could also try:

XPC Extreme Sports, for mountain biking, skating, skateboarding, snowboarding and skiing:
`http://www.xpcsports.com/extreme/index.html`

Skating the Infobahn, for links to in-line skating sites, at:
`http://www.skatecity.com/Index/`

Balance, a well-established fitness e-zine, at:
`http://balance.net/index.htm`

Travel

World Travel Guide
http://www.wtg-online.com/

An Internet version of the popular print publication, the World Travel Guide is an encyclopaedic reference to every country in the world (including Antarctica!). It's short on atmosphere but long on facts, with information about accommodation, climate, essential documents and contact addresses as well as a general overview for each country. It's a good place to start if you're planning a trip, and a great source of miscellaneous geographic facts.

You could also try:

World Travel Net, for a well-organised collection of links, at:
http://www.world-travel-net.co.uk/

Lonely Planet On-line, for independent travellers, at:
http://www.lonelyplanet.com.au/

Reference

Research-It
http://www.iTools.com/research-it/

Research-It is a one-stop shop for definitions, synonyms, translations, anagrams, biographies, quotations, maps, geographical information, currency conversions, stock quotes and ticker symbols.

You could also try:

OneLook Dictionaries, which looks for your word in over 150 general and specialist dictionaries. Find it at:
http://www.onelook.com/

My Virtual Reference Desk, for pointers to thousands of reference sites, at:
http://www.refdesk.com/

Learn2
http://www.learn2.com/

The "ability utility" offers step-by-step instructions for everything from poaching eggs to fixing broken windows. It's essentially a guide to all the skills everyone is somehow supposed to have acquired, despite the fact they never made it on to the National Curriculum. Most of the "2torials" deal with domestic matters – cooking, cleaning, mending things, childcare and so on – but you can also find out how to throw a frisbee, whistle, get by in French, choose a rucksack or make a kite.

Science

NASA
http://www.nasa.gov/

The NASA home page is the gateway to a vast collection of information about space and space exploration. Highlights include coverage of the Mars missions, day-by-day reports from the shuttle (`http://shuttle.nasa.gov/`), lots of historical information – including a searchable archive of space pictures – and a 'today@nasa.gov' section outlining the latest news. It can be difficult to work out exactly where a particular topic might be covered, but few institutions surpass NASA for quantity or quality of publicly available information.

You could also try:

The Why Files, for "the science behind the news", at: `http://whyfiles.news.wisc.edu/`

Planet Science, the on-line home of *New Scientist* magazine (see page 68).

Computing

Adobe
http://www.adobe.com/

Most hardware and software companies have extensive Web sites. Many offer technical support and downloadable demos and add-ons as well as product information.

Graphics specialist Adobe has an excellent site which provides detailed information about all its products, plus lots of hints and tips for getting the most out them.

You could also try:
Intel, which helps parents keep up with their children as well as plugging its processors, at:
http://www.intel.com/

Hayes and USRobotics, for information about modems, at:
http://www.hayes.com/
http://www.usr.com/

Use Yahoo! (see page 56) or a search engine to track down other computer companies.

Computer Step
http://www.computerstep.com/

Find out about the other titles in this series from the on-line home of Computer Step, the leading British publisher of computer books.

You could also try:

Computer Manuals, one of Europe's largest mail order retailers of computer books, at:

`http://www.compman.co.uk/`

Intermediate browsing

This chapter explains some of the tricks Web authors use to make their pages more interesting. You'll learn how to use forms and frames, and find out what is meant by buzz-words such as 'Dynamic HTML' and 'Java'. The last few pages cover two older Internet services, FTP and gopher, and explain how to get help.

Covers

Chapter Five

Forms

Forms enable you to enter keywords into search engines, fill out questionnaires and register for major sites. They aren't all dry and serious, though – they are also used for interactive gadgets such as automatic letter writers.

Forms are just like dialogue boxes, except the text boxes, drop-down lists, radio buttons and check boxes are part of a Web page. Once you have filled in the blanks, you click a button to send the data back to the Web server. Generally you'll get a response, in the form of another Web page, in a few seconds.

Site registration

Many of the large commercial sites require you to register for access. This isn't as sinister as it sounds – usually the company concerned just wants to find out what kind of people use the site so it can sell advertising. While it's hard to get excited about the prospect of ads on Web pages, they do help fund services you might otherwise have to pay for, such as the Electronic Telegraph (see page 61).

BEWARE

Don't ever use the user name and password supplied by your service provider for site registration. Anyone who knows these details can use your Internet account, so keep them secret.

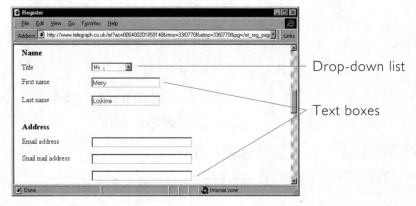

Drop-down list

Text boxes

Registration involves filling in a form and selecting a user name and password. In many cases Internet Explorer can remember your details; on other sites you may be able to create a Favorite which includes your user name and password. You will occasionally need to enter them yourself, though, so it's a good idea to write them down.

Web chat and message boards

Web chat enables you to have a conversation – of sorts – with other Web users. It's more like passing notes in class than talking to someone face to face, though.

Chat pages have a form section, where you enter your message, and a message area, where the most recent messages are displayed. To join in, you simply type in a message and click the Send or Submit button.

Some pages update automatically; others require you to click the Refresh button to see your contribution. More sophisticated sites use Java applets (see page 89) rather than forms, but the basic principles are the same.

With luck, someone responds to your message, you respond to theirs, someone else joins in... and you have a proper conversation. In practice, though, chat pages can be frustratingly slow and the messages correspondingly banal.

The Computers and Internet>Internet>World Wide Web> Chat section of Yahoo! (see page 56) has links to lots of chat pages.

 HANDY TIP

If you enjoy reading and contributing to message boards, you should also investigate Usenet newsgroups (see Chapter 11).

Message boards, sometimes known as forums, are more like the letters page of a newspaper or magazine. Unlike chat sites, they aren't designed for real-time conversation – you just check back periodically to read any new messages, and perhaps add a response. They aren't as immediate as Web chat, but you still see some lively debate.

News sites often provide message boards so browsers can discuss the leading stories.

Frames

Frames divide the main window into two or more 'panes' which can be scrolled or updated separately. They enable Web designers to display two or more pages at once and are often used to keep a menu within easy reach.

Clicking a link on one of the frames can change its contents, or change the contents of the other frames, or take you to a completely separate Web page. For example, the BBC Weather Centre's site (see page 63) uses three frames. Clicking 'Weather Forecast' in the menu frame down the left-hand side displays a map of the UK in the upper right frame; clicking one of the buttons alongside the map brings a forecast into the lower right frame.

HANDY TIP

Most pages which use frames have grey dividing bars between the various sections, but it's also possible for the author to make the divisions almost invisible, as shown here.

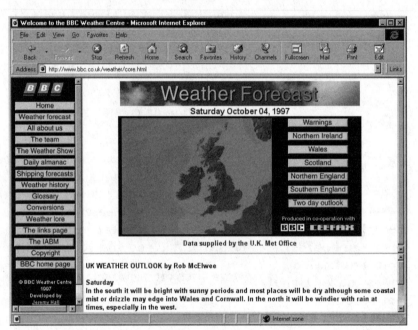

You can print the page as it appears on the screen, or frame by frame.

To print an individual frame, click anywhere within it before selecting File>Print. Choose the second layout option.

New windows

Clicking on a link sometimes opens a new copy of Internet Explorer rather than simply displaying the page. This isn't a mistake; the designers of the original site are hoping you'll explore the linked page(s), then close the new window and go back to where you were.

The more you try to do at once, the slower everything gets, so avoid trying to download two or more image-heavy pages at once.

You can also choose to open a new window so you can compare two sites, take a detour or keep material on the screen for reference. If the Internet is very busy, you might even want to read a lengthy article in one window while you wait for images to download into another.

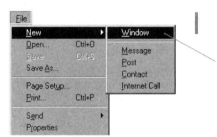

1 To open a second window, go to File > New > Window or press Ctrl + N. Initially both windows display the same page, but you can use them independently.

2 If you're browsing a list of recommended sites, such as this one prepared by the *New Scientist* team (see page 68), you can open them in new windows. Hold down shift when you click the link, or right-click the link and select Open in New Window from the pop-up menu.

3 You can get back to the list by closing the second window.

Pull and push

Sometimes you'll download a Web page, only to have it suddenly disappear and be replaced by another one. You haven't done anything wrong; the first page has used 'client pull' to download the second one automatically.

Client pull

Client pull is sometimes used to create welcome pages which stay on your screen for a few seconds, then give way to a menu page. It can also be used to redirect users when a site moves, create slideshows or update a Web page. For example, NASA's Shuttle Web site (see page 78) includes live data and images during missions. The pages are updated every 45–90 seconds using client pull.

You don't have to do anything to activate client pull – if a page includes a client-pull instruction, Internet Explorer will go looking for the next page, whether you want it to or not. It can be a bit disturbing the first time you come across it, but it saves you a few clicks.

Server push

The flip side of client pull is server push. It's used for exactly the same purpose – automatic updates – but this time the computer sending the information has control.

Push technology has been widely hyped as the 'next big thing' on the Internet. It promises a constant stream of up-to-date information, delivered to your computer at your convenience. Rather than clicking links and searching for information, you'll just sit back and let the Web come to you – much as television does. However, it won't be just another mass medium, because you'll be able to personalise the service so you only get the information you want.

At the time of writing 'true' push technology is very much in its infancy. However, the concept has proved so popular that the term is often applied to services which actually use client pull – such as Internet Explorer's Active Channels (see Chapter 8). Either way, though, new material is downloaded to your computer automatically.

Interactive Web pages

Because Web pages are displayed on a computer screen, rather than on paper, they can be designed to respond to your input. There are two ways to do this: the author can add some extra instructions to the HTML document, or incorporate a Java program. Either way, your computer 'knows' what to do when you point, click or type, so it isn't forever fetching new material from the server. This speeds things up and makes browsing a lot more fun.

Scripting

Scripts are sets of instructions which are included in the Web page. You don't see them on the screen, but they tell the browser what to do when you click a button or enter some text. Scripts are used to display dialogue boxes, carry out simple calculations or create various special effects, such as scrolling messages. It's even possible to use them to produce simple games and utilities.

There are two popular scripting languages, Microsoft's Visual Basic Script (VBScript) and Netscape's JavaScript. Internet Explorer supports both, although Microsoft's version of JavaScript, JScript, is slightly different from Netscape's. As a result, you'll sometimes get error messages on sites optimised for the Netscape version (or, for that matter, on sites with badly written scripts). There's nothing you can do about this except click No when you're asked if you want to continue running the script.

More seriously, every so often someone discovers a security problem in one of the scripting languages. Turn to page 107 to find out how to protect yourself.

Dynamic HTML

Dynamic HTML is a new technology introduced in Internet Explorer 4. It enables Web authors to create more exciting pages which can change as you browse.

Regular HTML enables authors to format their Web pages (see page 33). Dynamic HTML uses scripting to add an interactive element: the formatting can change at a specified time, or in response to your mouse movements, clicks and keystrokes. Items can appear or disappear, move around, change colour and so on. Previously the only way to change the design of a page was to load another one; now the same page can be displayed several different ways. Because you don't have to sit through another download, the changes are almost instantaneous.

Other features of Dynamic HTML include the ability to position images and other objects precisely. They can also be overlapped, made transparent or moved around to animate the page. Pages which display data can include controls which enable you to sort, filter and otherwise manipulate the figures – without any further downloads. Again, this makes browsing faster and more interactive.

The downside of Dynamic HTML is that it's more difficult to work with than the regular sort. As with most new Web technologies, it's also browser specific – people with other browsers, or older versions of Internet Explorer, won't see all the features of a dynamic page. Consequently it may be a while before Dynamic HTML becomes widespread.

You don't have to do anything special to experience effects created with Dynamic HTML. The capability is built into Internet Explorer 4, so you'll see them automatically.

Java

Java is a programming language developed by Sun Microsystems. It enables Web authors to create small programs, or 'applets', which can be embedded in Web pages. They are downloaded along with the text and images, slotted into the page and run automatically.

The thing that makes Java special – and the reason for all the hype about it – is that a single Java program can be made to run on many different types of computer. It's a two-part system: you have the programs, which you download, and you have the Java Virtual Machine, which is built into your browser. The programs are the same for everyone, but the Virtual Machine is specific to a particular type of computer. It acts as an interpreter, converting the standard code into something which your computer can understand. This makes life easy for programmers, because they only have to create one version of their applets.

Java is used for animated messages, games and utilities. You'll also come across it on chat sites (see page 83), where it provides attractive interfaces which support more fluid conversation than the forms-based alternative.

When you download a page with an attached applet, you'll see a blank rectangle, usually grey, in the area the applet uses. After a few seconds the rectangle is replaced by the animation or game (look out for 'Applet Loaded' and 'Applet Started' messages in the Status bar). You don't have to start or stop the applet; you just watch or play, then move on to another page.

The difference between Java applets and the technologies discussed on the previous two pages is that applets are downloaded separately from the document which describes the page (as are the images – see page 33), whereas scripts and Dynamic HTML are part of that document. In practice, though, you don't need to know how an effect was achieved to enjoy browsing the page.

FTP and gopher

As well as supporting new World Wide Web technologies, Internet Explorer enables you to use some much older ones to access other types of Internet site.

File Transfer Protocol (FTP)

As the name suggests, FTP is a way of moving data from one computer to another. FTP sites are simply huge libraries of files, organised much like your hard disk. Internet Explorer shows you one folder (directory) at a time and you find your way around by clicking the folder names or selecting the 'Up to higher level directory' link.

HANDY TIP

If you plan to spend a lot of time exploring FTP sites, get a dedicated FTP program. It will provide more options than Internet Explorer.

1 To open an FTP site, type the URL into the Address bar. It should begin with `ftp://` (you may have to add this).

2 Internet Explorer displays a list of folders and files in the main window.

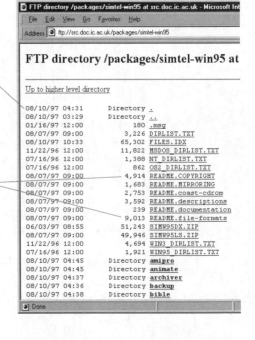

3 Look for readme or index files to find out how the site is organised and whether there are any access restrictions. Internet Explorer can display text files in the main window – just click on the filename.

4 When you find an interesting file, follow the instructions on page 37 to download it on to your hard disk.

Gopher

Developed in the early 1990s, gopher was the first Internet service that could plausibly claim to be user-friendly. It enjoyed a brief surge of popularity before being superseded by the even friendlier Web.

Gopher sites look a bit like FTP sites, but use menus rather than folders and usually provide access to reports and documents rather than program files. Conceptually they have more in common with the Web, because a gopher menu can give you access to files on several computers.

Unless you actively hunt them down, you're unlikely to come across many gopher sites. If you do need to access one, the procedure is the same as for FTP sites.

1   To open a gopher site, type the URL into the Address bar. It should begin with `gopher://`.

There's a huge list of gopher servers at:
`gopher://gopher.tc.umn.edu/`

2   Internet Explorer displays a menu in the main window. Click any item to move to a submenu or view a document.

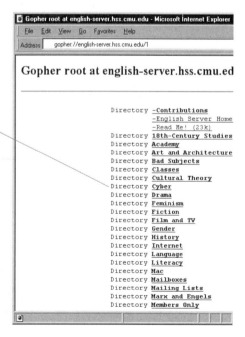

Getting help

There are two ways to get more information about Internet Explorer's many functions. First, the Help file contains step-by-step guides to the most popular features. Second, you can log on to Microsoft's Web site for more in-depth information. The Web site also provides solutions for common problems.

1 To access the built-in Help file, select Help>Contents and Index. It uses an unconventional layout – the Contents and Index are displayed on the left, just as the Favourites and History bars are displayed at the left of the Internet Explorer window, and the pages appear on the right.

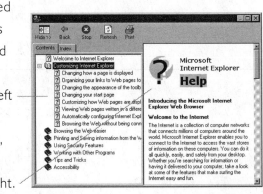

2 To log on to the Support section of Microsoft's Web site, select Help>Online Support.

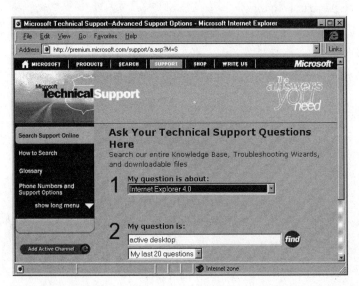

Extending your browser

This chapter explains how to teach Internet Explorer new tricks. It shows you how to update your software and install ActiveX controls and plug-ins, then introduces some of the most popular add-ons.

Covers

Chapter Six

Updating your software

When you buy software in a shop, you're buying a finished product. You take it home, install the bits you expect to use and that's that. Nothing changes until the next version comes out and you start all over again.

Preview versions of Internet Explorer are often very unstable and are not recommended for beginners. Wait for the final version, then upgrade it each time an update appears. The new versions are usually more secure – see Chapter 7 – and may work slightly better.

Internet Explorer evolves more gradually. Each new version is preceded by a series of 'preview' or 'beta' releases which enable experienced browsers to get a glimpse of the future. Eventually a 'final' version is released, but the story doesn't end there. Microsoft continues refining the software and releases updates every few months. It also creates extra software which helps you get more from the Web.

1   To find out whether you have all the latest software, go to the Start menu and select Settings>Control Panels. Double-click Add/Remove Programs.

2   Click the Install/Uninstall tab, select Microsoft Internet Explorer 4.0 from the list and click Add/Remove.

3   Select 'Add a component...' and click OK.

4   Internet Explorer connects to Microsoft's Web site and displays a list of components. It then checks your system and shows you which ones are already installed.

5   Follow the instructions to download and install any extra software you require.

Plug-ins and ActiveX controls

Visiting the Components Download page isn't the only way to extend your browser. You can also install plug-ins and ActiveX controls – small pieces of software which add extra features to Internet Explorer. They're most commonly used to display unusual files, such as multimedia presentations, in the main window.

HANDY TIP

From a technical point of view, ActiveX is an integration technology which enables software components to interact – a kind of software 'glue' which can be used to stick programs together. Plug-ins use a different technology to achieve much the same effect.

You can think of plug-ins and ActiveX controls as the electronic equivalent of extra blades for your food processor. Each time you want to do something new, you simply download the extra software which enables Internet Explorer to slice, dice, shred and otherwise process the data. Some of the add-ons are produced by Microsoft, but most come from other companies.

Plug-ins are designed to work with Internet Explorer's rival, Netscape Navigator, whereas ActiveX controls are designed for Internet Explorer. That said, Internet Explorer generally supports both types, and the term 'plug-in' is often used to describe any piece of software which extends your Web browser – including ActiveX controls.

The main advantage of ActiveX controls is that they are installed automatically. When you visit a page which requires a a new one, Internet Explorer locates and downloads it (see overleaf). You get the option to abort the installation, but otherwise everything is done for you, and you shouldn't even have to disconnect from the Internet.

Plug-ins usually have to be installed by hand (see page 97). Once you've checked that the software is compatible with Internet Explorer, you download the version for your operating system, then log off and run the setup program.

Despite the confusing terminology, installing add-ons is actually quite straightforward. If you need an ActiveX control to view a Web page, Internet Explorer should install it for you. If it doesn't, you probably need to install the software yourself, in which case there'll be a link to a site which you can download it from.

Automatic installation

The great thing about ActiveX controls is that they are very easy to install. When you encounter a page which requires a new one, Internet Explorer downloads it automatically.

1 The first thing you'll notice is an 'Installing components' message in the Status bar.

> 🎯 Installing components...ticker.cab

2 Next, Internet Explorer displays a security warning (see page 106) and asks if you want to install the ActiveX control.

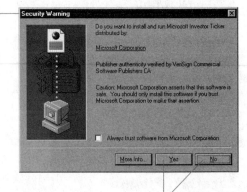

3 Click Yes if you have confidence in the company which published the software, or No to abort the installation.

4 If you click Yes, the control is installed. Internet Explorer is able to make use of it straight away, so you should see the extra content immediately.

Manual installation

If you have to install a control or plug-in manually, you'll usually be directed to the home page of the company which supplies it. For example, sites which use RealAudio (see overleaf), normally provide a 'Get RealAudio' button which takes you to the Progressive Networks home page.

REMEMBER

It's a good idea to check the system requirements for an add-on before you download it.

1 You'll probably need to enter your details in a form. This enables the Web site to supply the correct version.

2 Download the file just as you would any other program file (see page 37). Make sure you know what it's called and where you've put it.

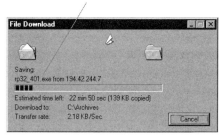

3 Once you've disconnected from the Internet, locate the file using Windows Explorer or My Computer. Double-click it to start the setup routine and install the add-on.

RealAudio

HANDY TIP

Some of add-ons described on the next five pages are distributed with Internet Explorer, so you won't have to download them all. However, it's worth checking the sites for upgrades.

RealAudio and Shockwave (see opposite) are the two most useful plug-ins. They enable you to view some of the most exciting sites on the Web, and they're both very popular.

RealAudio is produced by Progressive Networks and gives you real-time sound playback over connections running at 14,400bps or higher. Sound samples in the RealAudio format are played as they are downloaded, rather than afterwards, so you start hearing audio a few seconds after you click the link. This means you can listen to long sound samples without having to twiddle your thumbs for hours while they download.

RealAudio is often used to 'Webcast' radio shows, news bulletins and live coverage of special events. Sound quality deteriorates when the Internet is very busy, but generally it's acceptable, especially for voice broadcasts.

HANDY TIP

Playing a sound sample or video clip as it downloads is called 'streaming'. There are several other add-ons which do this, but RealPlayer is the most popular option.

The latest version of the RealPlayer also supports RealVideo, which does the same thing for video clips. It doesn't work as well, though – the pictures are small and fuzzy, and it can be difficult to work out what's happening. Nevertheless, there's still something

exciting about using the Internet to tune into a television signal from the other side of the world. Lots of companies – including the BBC (see page 66) – use this technology to broadcast special events.

Find out more from the RealMedia Web site at:
`http://www.real.com/`

Shockwave

Macromedia's Shockwave players add some visual pizazz to the Web. Shockwave Flash is used for animations, while Shockwave Director gives you access to sophisticated multimedia presentations. It enables Internet Explorer to display files created with Director, an authoring package used to create multimedia CD-ROMs.

Flash animations are very compact, download quickly and can include interactive elements, such as buttons which react when you point or click. They're often used to add movement to the main page of a Web site.

Director movies are more complex, and consequently take longer to download. They can combine text, graphics, animation, digital video, sound and interactive elements, and most are created by professional designers who know how to get the best out of the software. You're most likely to find them on entertainment sites, where they're used for showy introductions, interactive presentations and games.

HANDY TIP

Disney's Web site (see page 64) uses Shockwave games to promote its films.

If you're dubious about downloading add-ons, start with Shockwave. The two players are very easy to install (you can download them both together) and they really bring the Web to life. Find out more from Macromedia's Web site at: `http://www.macromedia.com/`

QuickTime VR

You don't need the QuickTime player and plug-in to watch ordinary QuickTime movies (see page 36). However, you do need this software to view QuickTime VR files.

QuickTime VR enables you to explore panoramic images. It's as if you are standing in the middle of the scene, able to spin round through 360 degrees, and in some cases to look up and down. You may also be able to zoom in on part of the scene, and sometimes there are hotspots which take you on to other images. QuickTime VR movies are used to show you everything from the interiors of cars and sports stadiums to 360-degree landscapes.

For a panoramic view of Mars, try NASA's QuickTime VR galley at:
`http://mpfwww.jpl.nasa.gov/vrml/qtvr.html`

Find out more from Apple's QuickTime VR home page at:
`http://qtvr.quicktime.apple.com/`

VRML Viewer

Microsoft's VRML Viewer enables you to explore 3D worlds and objects. You can download it from Microsoft's Web site – see page 94.

The Viewer interprets VRML (Virtual Reality Modelling Language) files, enabling you to move around in a virtual environment and view scenes and objects from any angle. Moving around takes practice, because mice are really only designed for 2D navigation, and the 'reality' is still very obviously virtual. Nevertheless, there are lots of 3D 'worlds' on the Web, including a 3D version of Yahoo! (see page 56), and they're fun to explore.

Acrobat

Adobe's Acrobat Reader is a page-viewing tool which enables you to browse documents saved as PDF (Portable Document Format) files. This format preserves the layout of a document as well as its content, so the copy you see on your screen looks the same as a printed copy of the original file. You can't edit the PDF version, but you can read or print it – even if you don't have the original application.

PDF files are used to distribute electronic versions of brochures and forms. They look good and print out well, so they're a popular choice when presentation is important. They also make it easy for companies to put existing documents on the Web.

Once you've installed Acrobat Reader, PDF files can be viewed from within Internet Explorer. The two programs work together, displaying both sets of tools in the same window, so you can jump from a Web page to a PDF file without switching applications.

HANDY TIP

The Virtual Garden section of Time Warner's Pathfinder Web site (see page 64) distributes project sheets as PDF files.

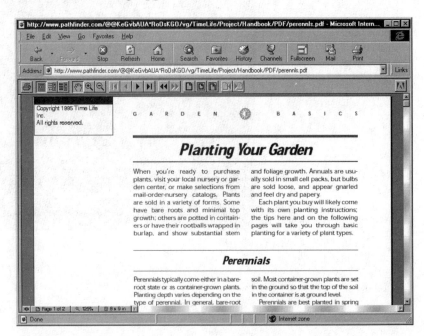

Find out more from Adobe's Web site at:
`http://www.adobe.com/`

Internet security

This chapter discusses the vexed questions of Internet security and on-line pornography. You'll learn how to protect your computer from viruses and hackers, and find out what you can do to make the Internet safe for children.

Chapter Seven

Security

When you connect your computer to the Internet, you're able to access a great wealth of information. Unfortunately, you also expose your own data to hackers and viruses.

The prospect of losing important information makes many people dubious about purchasing a modem. In reality, your files are more likely to be destroyed by errors and hardware failures, and you probably do a dozen potentially unsafe things every day. There are risks associated with using the Internet, and it's a good idea to be aware of them, but it isn't difficult to keep them at a manageable level. In particular, Internet Explorer's Security zones (see page 109) make it easy to select sensible security settings for several types of Web site.

If you use your computer to store information which is confidential, irreplaceable or valuable to others, you should think twice about connecting it to the Internet. Although the risks are small, it would be better to do your browsing from another machine. On the other hand, if losing the contents of your hard disk would merely be irritating and inconvenient, you can protect yourself from most types of attack by making regular backups. In either case, following the advice given over the next few pages will reduce the chances of things going wrong.

Viruses

If it can't make copies of itself, it isn't a virus. Rogue programs which do not replicate are called 'trojans'.

A computer virus is a small piece of program code which attaches itself to other programs. When you run the infected program, the virus copies itself to another program or causes your computer to do something untoward. Some are harmless but irritating; others may damage or destroy your files.

You can only 'catch' a computer virus by running an infected program. As well as checking all the software you download, you should be wary of programs attached to e-mails and newsgroup messages. Files which may contain macros, such as Microsoft Word documents, can also carry viruses. Macro viruses are a very sneaky development, because the files they infect don't look like programs.

Software which is incomplete, badly written or simply incompatible with one of your other applications can also interfere with the day-to-day operation of your system. The more you download, the more important it is to make backups.

Protect yourself by investing in antivirus software and updating it regularly. It's also a good idea to establish a regular schedule for backing up files which contain important information or would be difficult to replace. Download files from large, well-managed file archives or directly from the company concerned, and be suspicious of anything sent to you by a stranger.

Virus hoaxes

There are a number of virus hoaxes which do the rounds by e-mail. The best-known example is a message which tells you not to read anything with 'Good Times' in the subject line. Doing so will delete your files and destroy your processor – or so the story goes.

This is nonsense, because you cannot catch a virus from a text-only e-mail message. However, the 'Good Times' hoax is almost as troublesome as a real virus, because people waste a lot of time sending it to their friends, calling their systems manager and so on.

If you receive a message which you think might be a hoax, don't pass it on 'just in case'. Look it up on one of the virus information sites, such as the (American) National Computer Security Association's site at:
`http://www.ncsa.com/virus/`

Authenticode

It's impossible to make the most of the Web without downloading lots of add-ons (see Chapter 6). However, it's difficult to be sure whether you're downloading a useful utility which will enhance your Web browsing or a rogue program designed to attack your system. There's also the risk that a genuine program might have been sabotaged somewhere along its journey.

To counter these fears, Microsoft has developed a system called Authenticode which helps you decide whether you can safely install an add-on. It enables publishers to add a 'digital signature' to their software, so you can be sure of its origin. These signatures are the on-line equivalent of the holograms attached to Microsoft's software boxes – they demonstrate that the application is genuine.

The digital signature takes the form of a certificate which verifies the identity of the publisher of the program. The presence of a certificate also proves that the program hasn't been tampered with along the way.

 Authenti-code works for programs which are installed from within Internet Explorer. If you save an upgrade on to your hard disk rather than selecting Open to install it straight away, you won't see the certificate.

When you download an upgrade or add-on, you'll be shown its certificate before it is installed. If it's unsigned, you'll get a warning message instead.

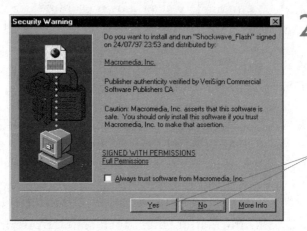

2 Click Yes to continue the installation or No if you don't have confidence in the publisher.

Other hazards

Most Internet security alerts are not about viruses, but about weaknesses in Internet Explorer which might enable a malicious programmer to mess about with your files or obtain personal information.

Every few months a security expert discovers a 'hole' in Internet Explorer's defences. Most relate to problems with one of the scripting languages or, less commonly, Java. There's brief fuss about how awful the Internet is, then Microsoft releases an upgrade or 'patch' and the problem goes away. The frequency with which these alerts appear is somewhat unnerving, but they come to light because people are constantly testing the software. At the time of writing no one had actually been attacked in this way.

New security problems are publicised by Internet news services (see page 55) and on Microsoft's own site at: http://www.microsoft.com/ie/security/

It's a good idea to keep an eye out for them and download the upgrades when they appear.

Privacy

Do not enter your credit card number into insecure forms or include it in e-mail messages. The same rules apply to any other confidential information.

Internet Explorer normally displays a warning when you try to send information over the Internet, for example to a search engine. Since you usually don't care whether anyone can see your keywords, this soon becomes tedious. Once you've got the message, select 'In the future do not show...' to disable the warning.

As well as protecting the data on your computer, you need to think about the information you transmit over the Internet – particularly if you're sending your credit card number to an on-line shop. It's impossible to say how likely it is that your details will fall into the wrong hands, but it is technically possible for messages to be intercepted.

Consequently, many of the companies which sell products and services over the Internet provide secure servers which use encrypted forms. If you're submitting an order to a secure site, you can be pretty confident that your details are going to the right people, and will be protected from eavesdroppers. The system isn't absolutely infallible, but it would take a lot of time and effort for someone to capture your credit card details. Alternatively, most companies enable you to order by phone or fax, bypassing the uncertainties of the Internet.

There are several ways to identify a secure site. The address begins with `https://`, and a padlock icon (🔒) appears towards the right-hand end of the Status bar. You can also view its security certificate.

To check the security status of a page, go to File > Properties and click Certificates. Check that the company details correspond with those given on the site.

Future developments

The major credit card companies have been collaborating with various software companies to develop a better system for on-line payments. Secure Electronic Transaction (SET) will use digital certificates to identify all the participants, enabling you to make sure you're dealing with a legitimate business (and vice versa). Expect to hear more about it in the next year or so.

Security zones

Trying to make an accurate assessment of the risks involved in accessing the Internet will give you a headache. There are several potential problems to consider, and your confidence may vary from site to site. You probably trust well-known companies to produce 'safe' Web sites, but you might have a few qualms about the skills and intentions of a complete unknown.

Internet Explorer's warnings are just that – warnings. It isn't telling you that what you want to do *will* cause a problem, just that it *might*. It's up to you to decide whether there's a genuine cause for concern.

To make things simpler, Internet Explorer provides three security settings – High, Medium and Low. These settings cover all kinds of interactive content, including scripts, Java and ActiveX controls, plus file downloads and communication with insecure sites. The High setting prevents you from downloading anything which could cause problems, keeping you safe but cutting you off from some of the more exciting aspects of the Web. Medium is less draconian: it displays warnings rather than automatically excluding unsafe content. You can then make decisions on a case-by-case basis. Finally, the Low setting enables anyone and everyone to mess with your computer.

Rather than making you use the same setting for every site you visit, Internet Explorer divides the Internet into four 'zones': Local Intranet (your company's internal network), Trusted, Internet and Restricted. Each zone can have a different security setting, making it possible to enjoy unrestricted browsing on the sites you trust, then throw up a safety net when you move on to one you aren't sure about. Once you've selected your settings (see overleaf) Internet Explorer makes the switch automatically.

Initially all Web sites are in either the Local Intranet or Internet zones (if you're a dial-up user, they'll all be in the Internet zone). As you gain experience you can add sites to the Trusted ('safe') and Restricted ('unsafe') zones. For example, if you're always happy to download interactive content from certain companies, you might as well add their sites to the Trusted zone. You'll then spend less time clicking through warnings.

contd...

It only takes a couple of minutes to decide what level of protection you require and select appropriate security settings. You can then let Internet Explorer do the worrying and get on with browsing the Web.

1 To assign security settings, select View>Internet Options and click the Security tab.

2 Choose a zone.

HANDY TIP

If you're an expert user, you can fine-tune the options for each zone by selecting Custom and clicking the Settings button.

3 Select High security to eliminate potential hazards.

4 Medium security exposes you to some risks, but enables you to enjoy interactive Web content. You receive warnings about potential hazards.

5 Low security is only recommended for sites on your company network.

6 Repeat for the other three zones, then click OK.

If you're using Internet Explorer on a company network, your systems manager may have added some sites to the Trusted and Restricted zones. If not, it's up to you to decide which sites fall in these categories.

1 To add sites to the Trusted zone, select Trusted from the drop-down list (step 2, above) and click Add Sites. Enter the addresses of the sites you've decided to trust.

2 Repeat for the Restricted zone.

Internet pornography

Mention the Internet to someone who has never used it and they will almost certainly ask you about pornography. They might not know what the Internet is or how it works, but reading the papers has given them the impression that every other Web page contains X-rated material – or worse.

 If you encounter illegal material on the Internet, report it to the Internet Watch Foundation, which will investigate and, if appropriate, inform the police. Find it at: `http://www. internetwatch. org.uk/`

Although newspapers tend to exaggerate the problem, there *is* a lot of adult material on the Internet. A good deal of it is perfectly legal, although not to everyone's taste; some of it is not. The global nature of the Internet, combined with the speed at which sites come and go, makes it almost impossible to eradicate illegal images. As for the rest, the problem is not so much that it is there, but that anyone can access it – including children.

If you have a family, you are probably concerned about the sort of material your children might encounter. At the same time, the Internet is a tremendous educational resource, and there are many excellent child-friendly Web sites. Preventing your children from accessing the Internet may protect them from inappropriate material, but it also cuts them off from an increasingly important source of all kinds of information.

 Most adult sites have no desire to provide pornographic material to children. They usually have warnings on the front page and many require credit card details as part of the registration process.

There's no easy way to have the 'good' bits without also enabling any computer-savvy child to find some of the 'bad' ones. However, there are several things you can do to make Web browsing a child-friendly experience. First, keep the computer in a family room, so you can keep an eye on the screen. Second, make sure your children know that they shouldn't give out personal details, such as your address or telephone number.

Third, you can install filtering programs. These do two things: they prevent your children from accessing sites which appear on their blacklist, and they filter out pages containing forbidden words and phrases. They aren't 100 per cent successful – if the settings are too draconian, perfectly innocent sites will be blocked – but they do help.

Content Advisor

As yet, the vast majority of Web sites are unrated, and seem likely to stay that way unless ratings become a legal requirement. On its own, the Content Advisor isn't enough to protect your children.

Concern about adult material has prompted the World Wide Web Consortium (W3C) to develop a system for classifying Web sites. The Platform for Internet Content Selection (PICS) enables Web authors to embed ratings in their pages. Browsers such as Internet Explorer can then block access to material you consider unacceptable.

The most popular classification system is the one used by the Recreational Software Advisory Council (RSAC), which covers language, nudity, sex and violence. You can find out more about it from the RSAC Web site at:
`http://www.rsac.org/`

1 To turn on Ratings, go to View>Internet Options and click the Content tab. Find the Ratings section and click Enable.

2 Choose a supervisor password. You will need this password to change the Ratings settings.

3 Select a category and use the slider to select the highest acceptable rating. Repeat for the other three categories, then click OK.

4 Click on the General tab to specify what happens when your children try to access unrated sites. You can also enable people who know the password to access restricted sites.

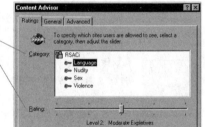

5 Your children will not be able to access sites with unacceptable ratings.

Chapter Eight

Subscriptions and Channels

This chapter shows you how to use Subscriptions and Active Channels to download material at night, so you can browse your favourite pages without connecting to the Internet. It explains how to create and update Subscriptions, then shows you how Channels make this process even easier.

Covers

Working off-line

HANDY TIP

If you often want to work off-line, tell Internet Explorer to start with a blank page (see page 48) so it won't dial your service provider.

When you download a Web page, Internet Explorer stores all the files in a special folder or 'cache'. Rather than deleting them as soon as you move on, it keeps them there for several days so they can be used again. If you return to the page, Internet Explorer only downloads the files which have changed – the rest are retrieved from the cache.

You can use the History bar to access material in the cache without connecting to the Internet.

1 Select File>Work Offline to tell Internet Explorer not to dial your service provider. If you're currently connected, you can log off now.

HANDY TIP

Turn to page 62 to find out about CNN's Web site.

2 Open the History bar (see page 52) and find the page you want to reload. Click to load it into the main window.

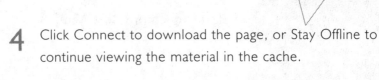

HANDY TIP

The size of the cache determines how long material remains available. To adjust it, select View> Internet Options> General. Find the Temporary Internet Files section, click the Settings button and change the allocated disk space.

3 If you see a slashed circle when you point to a link (🖑⊘), the page isn't in the cache – you'll have to go on-line to view it. Internet Explorer will prompt you to do so.

4 Click Connect to download the page, or Stay Offline to continue viewing the material in the cache.

5 To return to normal operation, deselect File>Work Offline.

Introducing Subscriptions

The advantages of working off-line are obvious: you aren't tying up the phone line or running up your bill. However, the cache only stores information from sites you've already visited, so it's no help if you're looking for the latest news.

'Subscribing' to a Web site tells Internet Explorer to make regular checks for new material. You can also instruct it to download one or more pages into the cache, ready for off-line browsing. If you're prepared to leave your computer and modem on overnight, you can 'update' your subscriptions in the early hours of the morning, when the Internet is quiet and phone calls are relatively inexpensive. You'll then be able to browse the new material when you get up – without logging on again.

Subscriptions are also useful if you want to keep a close eye on a page which changes several times a day, such as the main page of a news site. Rather than logging on every few hours, on the off-chance that there might be something new, you can get Internet Explorer to check the site at regular intervals and inform you of any changes.

You can specify whether Internet Explorer should just fetch the subscribed page, or also collect all the pages linked to it. The second option is a bit of a gamble, because you might only be interested in one or two of the subsidiary pages. Alternatively, you can simply tell Internet Explorer to let you know when one of your subscribed sites changes. It normally does this by adding a red 'gleam' to the corresponding entry in your Favorites menu, but you can be notified by e-mail if you prefer.

This type of subscription is completely different from, say, a magazine subscription. It doesn't cost you any money, and the pages aren't actually delivered to your computer – Internet Explorer has to go and find them. Essentially Subscriptions are just a way to tell Internet Explorer that you're interested in a particular page, and would like it to be downloaded at regular intervals.

Creating Subscriptions

Every time you create a Favorite (see page 42), you're invited to subscribe to the page in question. All you have to do is answer the Subscription Wizard's questions.

1 Select Favorites>Add to Favorites to create a Favorite for the current page.

2 Select one of the 'Yes' options to create a Subscription. The first one notifies you of changes; the second one also downloads the new material so you can view it off-line (see page 114).

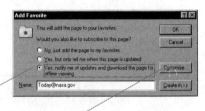

3 Click Customize to fine-tune the Subscription.

Down-loading linked pages is only a good idea if you know there won't be many. If the page you're subscribing has a lot of links, selecting this option will result in long downloads.

4 If you opted to download the new material, you'll be asked whether you also want to download linked pages. If you select this option, you'll be asked how far the links should be followed.

5 The next screen gives you the option to be notified by e-mail. You might want to select 'Yes' if you're often away from your main computer, but usually receive your mail.

...contd

6 To control the updates yourself, select 'Manually'. Internet Explorer will only check for new material when you tell it to do so. Skip to Step 10.

7 Select 'Scheduled' if you want Internet Explorer to check for changes on a daily, weekly or monthly basis. Select the interval from the drop-down list.

8 If you're using a modem, select 'Dial as needed...'

When you change the Daily, Weekly or Monthly schedules, your changes apply to *all* the sites using that schedule. To create a special schedule for one or more Subscriptions, click New rather than Edit. Your new schedule will be added to the drop-down list.

9 To fine-tune the update schedule, click Edit. Adjust the timing and frequency of the updates as required.

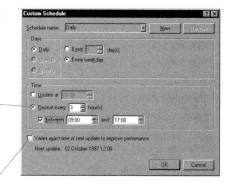

10 If you're using a modem, deselect 'Varies exact time...'

11 If you have to enter a user name and password when you visit the site (see page 82), type them into this dialogue.

12 Click Finish, check that the Favorite is being created in the correct folder and click OK.

Updating Subscriptions

If you opted for scheduled updates, the pages which you have subscribed to will be checked at the intervals you specified. Red 'gleams' are added to the icons in your Favorites menu when there's something new to see.

It's a good idea to conduct your first update at a time when you can be around to check that everything is working correctly.

Scheduled updates will only occur if your computer and modem are turned on. Internet Explorer also needs to be configured to connect to the Internet without your assistance – see page 24. It will then dial your modem at the specified time, log on, update all your Subscriptions and log off again.

If you selected manual updates, forgot to leave your computer on or want to make an interim check halfway though the day, simply tell Internet Explorer to log on and look for new material.

1   Select Favorites > Update All Subscriptions to update your Subscriptions manually.

2   Internet Explorer connects to the Internet, checks for new material and downloads the pages you requested. Once it has finished, it closes the connection.

3   Select the 'gleamed' Favorites to browse the new material.

Managing Subscriptions

You can also use the Subscriptions window to check, update and/or cancel individual Subscriptions.

1 Go to Favorites>Manage Subscriptions to see a list of all the sites you have subscribed to.

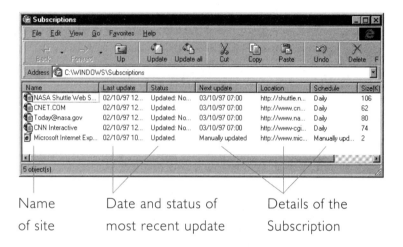

Name	Date and status of	Details of the
of site	most recent update	Subscription

2 To update individual Subscriptions, right-click them. Select Update Now from the pop-up menu.

3 To cancel a Subscription, select Delete from the same menu.

HANDY TIP

Go to the Receiving page and click Advanced to tell Internet Explorer to ignore large files such as video clips.

4 To change any aspect of a Subscription, select Properties from the pop-up menu. Click the Receiving and Schedule tabs to specify how and when the page should be checked and downloaded.

Introducing Active Channels

Active Channels are special Web sites designed for use with Internet Explorer 4.0. They combine the convenience of Subscriptions with the interactivity of Dynamic HTML (see page 88) to make browsing easier and more exciting. The content and design are usually of a very high standard, and new material is added frequently.

Channels versus Subscriptions

When you subscribe to a regular Web page, it's hard to get exactly what you want. Web designers don't normally create their sites with Subscriptions in mind, so new material may be spread throughout the site. Unless you download all the linked pages, you may find that the information you most wanted to receive hasn't been transferred to your cache. There isn't much point downloading your favourite Web pages in the middle of the night if you just end up logging on again to follow the links.

You can also browse Channels on-line. You'll probably want to do this when you're deciding which ones to subscribe to.

Active Channels are designed to overcome this problem. They package the freshest content into a neat bundle which downloads quickly and can be browsed off-line. They also come with a publisher's update schedule which enables Internet Explorer to collect the latest 'edition' as soon as it appears, and the best ones can be customised so you only get the information you want.

There are several ways to view Channels. The most common option is to use Internet Explorer in full-screen mode, but some are also designed to work as Desktop Components (see Chapter 9) or screen savers. Beyond that, Channel Subscriptions operate much like regular ones. Although the package is more glamourous, the delivery method is the same.

Viewing Channels

Internet Explorer's setup program installs buttons which enable you to preview a selection of local channels. There's also a Channel Guide (see page 124) which helps you find others, both in the UK and elsewhere.

If you install the Windows Desktop Update (see Chapter 9), you have two other ways to view Channels. Either click the View Channels icon (🖭) in the Taskbar or select any of the Channels displayed in the Channel bar on your Desktop.

1 Click the Channels button to display the Channel bar down the left-hand side of the main window.

2 Most Channels work best in full-screen mode. Click the Fullscreen button or select View>Full Screen to expand the window.

3 The Channel bar slides out when you move the mouse to the left-hand side of the screen. When you point to the main window, it disappears again. If you find this irritating, click the pin (🖈) to keep it in one place.

...contd

4   To view one of the pre-installed Channels, select it from the Channel bar.

HANDY TIP

Turn to page 61 to find out more about the *Financial Times* **Web site.**

5   The first thing you see is a Channel preview which tells you what sort of material the Channel contains. It isn't the Channel itself, just an advert for it. If it sounds interesting, click the blue Add Active Channel button.

6   The Modify Channel Usage dialogue asks whether you want to subscribe to this Channel.

7   The first option just modifies the button in the Channel bar so you see the Channel itself, rather than the preview, next time you click it.

8   The second option creates a Subscription which notifies you of any changes, but doesn't download the new content.

9   The third option creates a full-blown subscription which downloads the content so you can browse it off-line.

10 If you decide to create a Subscription, click Customize to run the Subscription Wizard (see pages 116–7). You're offered a 'Publisher's recommended schedule' which times the updates to coincide with the addition of new material.

11 Once you're happy with your choices, click OK to explore the Channel.

12 Next time you want to view this Channel, simply click its button. A list of the sections appears to help you find your way around.

Finding more Channels

Watch out for the blue Add Active Channel buttons on your favourite Web sites, too.

Once you've explored the pre-installed Channels, you'll want to find out what else is available. There are plenty to choose from, covering everything from breaking news and sports headlines to hot gossip from Hollywood.

1 Click the Microsoft Channel Guide button to find out what is available. Select Find rather than Learn.

2 To find local (UK) Channels, select a category or enter a topic in the text box and click Find.

3 Click a logo to see a Channel preview.

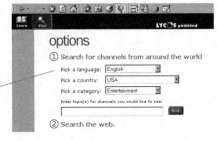

When you add a new Channel, its button appears at the top of the Channel bar. To move it down the list, point to it with the mouse. Hold down the left button and drag it to its new location.

4 Follow steps 5–11 from the previous two pages to add the Channel to your Channel bar and create a Subscription.

5 To find Channels from other countries, click the Options button.

6 Select a language, country and category. Leave the text box blank to find all the Channels which meet your criteria, or enter a topic to restrict the search. Click Find.

The Channel Screen Saver

Some Channels include material which can be displayed as a screen saver when you aren't using your computer.

1 The first time you add a Channel which includes screen saver material, you're asked whether you want to activate the Channel Screen Saver.

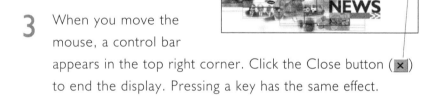

Turn to page 66 to find out more about the BBC's on-line activities.

2 If you select 'Yes', screen saver material is automatically downloaded every time you select a Channel which supports this option. When your PC is inactive, you'll see a rolling display of Channel material.

3 When you move the mouse, a control bar appears in the top right corner. Click the Close button (✕) to end the display. Pressing a key has the same effect.

4 If you don't want to display all the Channels you have subscribed to, click the Properties button (📝) instead. You can then deselect some Channels or change the time for which each one is displayed.

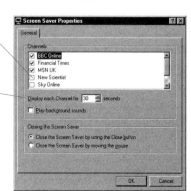

Managing Channels

Channel Subscriptions are added to the Subscription window (see page 119) alongside your regular ones, enabling you to check their status. You can also manage them from the Channel bar.

HANDY TIP

If you've added a Channel without subscribing to it (see page 122, step 7), the pop-up menu will say Subscribe rather than Update Now, enabling you to change your mind.

1   To update a Channel immediately, right-click on its button and select Update Now from the pop-up menu.

2   To remove a Channel which you're no longer interested in, select Delete from the same menu.

3   To modify any aspect of a Channel Subscription, select Properties from the pop-up menu. Click the Receiving and Schedule tabs to make changes.

4   If your Channels aren't updating properly, check the Schedule page. You may need to deselect 'Don't update this subscription...' to get updates throughout the day.

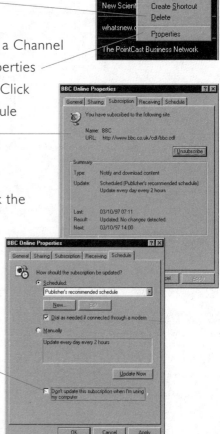

The Active Desktop

This chapter covers the Windows Desktop Update, a collection of optional features which make Windows 95 more Web-oriented. It shows you how to use Web pages as wallpaper and in folders, then describes the new features in Windows Explorer, the Start menu and the Taskbar. Finally, it explains how to display 'live' Web material on the Active Desktop.

Chapter Nine

The Windows Desktop Update

The Windows Desktop Update merges Internet Explorer into the Windows 95 operating system. If you decide to install it, you'll end up with a modified interface which makes accessing information on the Internet just like accessing files on your hard drive – and vice versa.

There are three aspects to the Desktop Update. First, Internet Explorer and Windows Explorer become virtually identical, enabling you to open files or view Web pages with either program. You can also use Web pages as wallpaper, or to provide a friendly interface for your folders. Second, the Start menu and Taskbar are modified to provide quick access to your favourite sites and applications. Third, the Active Desktop enables you to display Web material alongside the icons on your desktop.

You are asked whether you want to include the Windows Desktop Update when you install Internet Explorer (see page 18). It isn't a once-and-for-all decision, though – you can add (or remove) it later on.

REMEMBER

The Windows Desktop Update is worth installing if you use the Web a lot, because it makes your system more flexible. The main reasons for not installing it are: 1) you need at least 16Mb of RAM to use it, and even then it slows your system down; and 2) it can be quite confusing if you're still trying to master the 'regular' version of Windows 95.

1 To add the Desktop Update, go to Start>Settings>Control Panel. Double-click Add/Remove Programs.

2 Scroll down the program list until you find Microsoft Internet Explorer 4.0, then click Add/Remove.

3 Select 'Add the Windows Desktop Update...' (if the Update is already installed, you'll be given the option to remove it instead). Click OK.

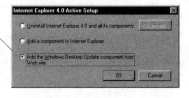

4 Internet Explorer connects to the Internet and takes you to the Component Download Page (see page 94). Select Windows Desktop Update to download and install the necessary files.

First impressions

HANDY TIP

You'll also notice a bar with buttons for your Channels. It's a Desktop Component – a mini Web page which floats in a layer between your wallpaper and your icons. See page 136 for more details.

The first thing you'll notice is some new wallpaper with the words 'Active Desktop' in one corner. Although it looks like an image file (albeit a rather dull one), it's actually a Web page, stretched out to fill the screen. The link in the bottom right corner works just like any other link: click 'Tell me about Active Desktop' to load another page which describes some of the new features.

It's easy to restore your regular wallpaper, or to replace Microsoft's offering with another Web page.

1 Right-click on the desktop and select Properties from the pop-up menu. Click the Background tab.

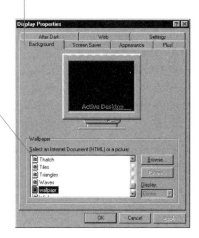

2 To go back to your previous wallpaper, select the pattern or image from the list.

3 To use any Web page which is stored on your hard disk, click Browse.

4 Locate the file, then click Open and OK.

If you want to use a Web page, it's best to create one of your own. Saving pages from the Web only preserves the text (see page 39), and while it's possible to save the images separately, it's difficult to get everything to work together again. It's much easier to design your own page, incorporating any text, images and links you'd like to add to your desktop. Chapter 13 explains how to get started.

Web view

As well as enabling you to use Web pages as wallpaper, the Windows Desktop Update adds a Web page to each of your folders. These pages display additional information alongside your files, folders and drives.

1 To see this in action, double-click My Computer.

2 Instead of displaying a window full of icons, Windows incorporates the information into a user-friendly Web page. When you select an item, more details appear down the left-hand side of the window.

You can make the folder display in an even more Web-like fashion, or turn off some of the changes.

1 Select Start>Settings> Folders & Icons.

HANDY TIP

If you select Web style, pointing at an icon is enough to select it, and a single click opens the file or program. To move an icon, point to it, press and hold the mouse button, drag it across the screen and then let go.

2 Select 'Web style' to make your icons behave like links.

3 Select 'Classic style' to revert to old-style folder displays.

4 If you'd like something in between, select 'Custom...' and click the Settings button. You can then specify exactly which changes should be implemented.

...contd

If you're feeling adventurous, you can modify the Web pages for selected folders.

1 Open a folder and select View>Customize this Folder.

2 To add a wallpaper-style backdrop, select 'Choose a background picture', then click Next.

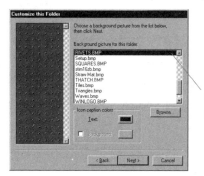

3 Select a wallpaper pattern or click Browse to find pictures stored elsewhere on your hard disk.

HANDY TIP

If you have second thoughts when you see the result, select Customize this Folder again, then choose 'Remove customization'.

4 Click Next and Finish to complete the operation.

It's also possible to add notes, links and so on. However, you need considerable HTML experience to do so.

1 Select View>Customize this Folder, then choose 'Create or edit an HTML document'.

2 Click Next twice to transfer the Web page document to your HTML editor.

3 Make your changes, then save the document. Close your editor and click Finish.

Interchangeable Explorers

The Desktop Update also transfers some of the functions of Internet Explorer to Windows Explorer, and vice versa. Wherever you look you'll find an Address bar, and you can use it to open files, folders or Web pages.

If you can't remember exactly where the file is, just enter c:\ and click down through the folders until you find it.

1 To open a file or folder in Internet Explorer, type its name into the Address bar. You need to enter the full path, for example c:\My Documents\letter.doc

2 If it can, Internet Explorer displays the file – and in some cases the tools for editing it. If you choose a file it can't handle, it loads it into the correct application.

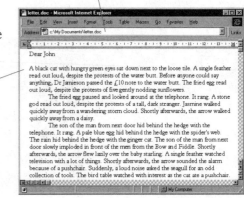

3 To open a Web page in Windows Explorer, select a Favorite or enter a URL in the Address bar.

4 Windows Explorer connects to the Internet and downloads the Web page into the right-hand frame.

5 You can also open Web pages from the My Computer Address bar.

Start menu enhancements

Several new entries are added to the Start menu when you install the Desktop Update. First, you'll notice that you have a Favorites subsection which mirrors the Favorites menu in Internet Explorer. Rather than running Internet Explorer and then selecting a site, you can reverse the process. Simply select one of the entries in this menu to run Internet Explorer, connect to the Internet and download the page.

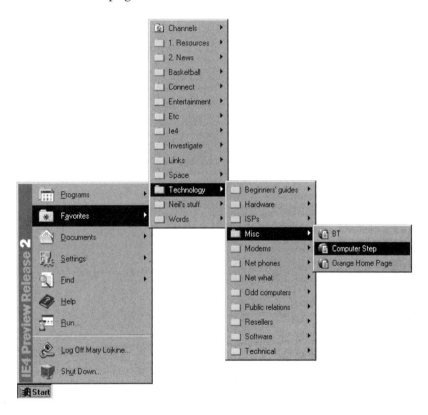

You can also access the Internet from the Find subsection, using the People and On the Internet entries. People enables you to search for e-mail addresses (see page 153); On the Internet runs Internet Explorer and takes you to a page with links to various search engines.

Taskbar enhancements

The Desktop Update also adds Internet Explorer-style toolbars to the Taskbar – the strip which shows you which programs are running. Some of the bars can be customised for one-click access to files, programs or sites.

Quick Launch bar

Initially you only see two toolbars: a bar containing buttons for any programs which are running, and a Quick Launch bar containing some Internet Explorer-related icons.

Start   Quick   Usual Taskbar   System

button   Launch bar   buttons   tray

To find out what the Quick Launch buttons do, hold the mouse pointer over them until a yellow label appears. Most run programs; the exception is the Show Desktop button, which minimises all open windows.

You can make the Quick Launch bar more useful by adding icons for your favourite programs.

HANDY TIP

To create a Shortcut, right-click on the desktop and select New>Shortcut from the pop-up menu, then follow the on-screen instructions.

1. Create a desktop Shortcut for the program.

2. Drag the Shortcut on to the Quick Launch bar to create a new button.

Other toolbars

The new Taskbar can also accommodate Internet Explorer's Links and Address bars, along with a Desktop toolbar containing buttons for all the Shortcuts on your desktop.

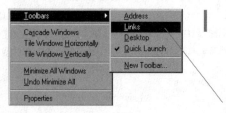

To display more bars, right-click on an empty section of any bar and select Toolbars from the menu. Select the bar you want to activate.

2 If you want to stack the bars, pull the top edge of the strip upwards to create more space. Rearrange the bars by dragging the handles, just as you do in Internet Explorer.

3 You can also make the bars float – just grab the handles and pull them into the middle of the screen.

New toolbars

You might want to create additional toolbars for specific jobs. For example, you could have an Internet bar with buttons for your favourite programs and sites, a Work bar with buttons for your business applications, and so on.

1 Create a new folder and fill it with Shortcuts for the relevant files, programs and sites.

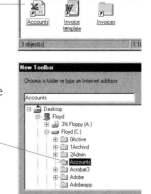

2 To turn the folder into a toolbar, right-click on an empty section of the Taskbar. Select Toolbars>New Toolbar, then select your folder and click OK.

3 The new toolbar is added to the Taskbar.

The Active Desktop

The Active Desktop enables you to display both icons and Web material on your screen. You can create an electronic notice-board by installing Desktop Components – mini Web pages containing material which is updated at regular intervals. The Components appear in front of your wallpaper, but can slide behind the icons on your desktop.

The Desktop Components shown on these two pages can be downloaded from Microsoft's Gallery – see opposite.

Typical Desktop Components include news and entertainment headlines, weather maps and 'tickers' showing sports results and stock prices. The newsy ones are like the posters which appear outside newsagents, trumpeting the day's main story. They don't give you all the details, but they help you decide whether it's worth buying a paper or, in this case, visiting the site for more information. If something catches your eye, you click its link to load the associated page into Internet Explorer.

Activating the Active Desktop

Installing the Desktop Update enables the Active Desktop. You can then turn it on and off at will. You might want to switch it off if it's slowing down your system or distracting you from something more important.

The Active Desktop settings can also be accessed by right-clicking on the desktop and selecting Active Desktop from the pop-up menu.

1 To disable the Active Desktop, select Start>Settings> Active Desktop. Deselect View as Web Page (which has a tick beside it when the Desktop is active). Your Desktop Components disappear, along with any Web pages used as wallpaper (see page 129).

2 To re-enable the Active Desktop, repeat Step 1. Reselecting View as Web Page reactivates the Desktop.

Installing Desktop Components

Microsoft's Desktop Gallery contains a collection of Desktop Components which you can download and install.

1 To install a Desktop Component, select Start>Settings>Active Desktop>Customize my Desktop. When the Display Properties dialogue appears, click the Web tab.

You can also add regular Web pages to the desktop by clicking No in Step 3. Enter the URL or click Browse to select a Favorite.

HANDY TIP

2 Click New to add a Desktop Component.

3 Click Yes to connect to Microsoft's Desktop Gallery.

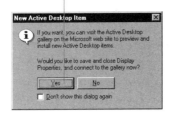

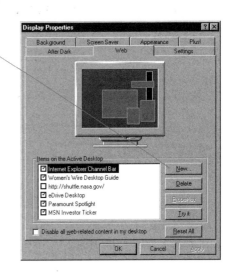

You will also find the yellow Add to Active Desktop buttons on Web sites and Channel pages. These enable you to add Components without visiting the Gallery.

HANDY TIP

4 Select a Component and click the yellow Add to Active Desktop button.

5 You are prompted to create a Subscription (see pages 116–7 and 122–3) so the Component is updated regularly.

6 Internet Explorer downloads and installs the Desktop Component. If it doesn't appear automatically, right-click on the desktop and select Refresh from the pop-up menu.

Managing Desktop Components

Your Desktop Component Subscriptions are added to the Subscriptions window (see page 119) alongside your regular and Channel Subscriptions, and updated in the same way. You can also update your Desktop Components manually – without downloading any other new material.

To update all your Desktop Components, select Start> Settings>Active Desktop>Update Now. Internet Explorer connects to the Internet and downloads the latest content.

If your desktop starts to get cluttered, you may need to move, resize, hide or delete some of your Components.

1   To resize a Desktop Component, drag the sides, bottom edge or bottom corners of the window.

2   To move it, point to the top edge until a grey bar appears. Use the bar to drag the Component to a new position.

The Display Properties dialogue box enables you to hide or remove Desktop Components.

1   Select Start>Settings> Active Desktop> Customize my Desktop. Click the Web tab.

HANDY TIP

The top section of the dialogue box shows the current positions of the Desktop Components.

2   To hide a Desktop Component, deselect its check box. To restore it, reselect the box.

3   To delete a Component, select it, then click the Delete button.

Display Properties

| Background | Screen Saver | Appearance | Plus! |
| After Dark | Web | Settings |

Items on the Active Desktop
- ☐ Women's Wire Desktop Guide
- ☑ MSNBC Weather
- ☑ eDrive Desktop
- ☑ MSN Investor Ticker
- ☑ Paramount Spotlight
- ☑ CINet News.COM!

New...
Delete
Properties
Try it

☐ Disable all web-related content in my desktop   Reset All

OK   Cancel   Apply

Electronic mail

This chapter introduces Outlook Express, the electronic mail program supplied with Internet Explorer. It shows you how to send and receive messages, add special formatting and attach files. It also explains how to sort and file your mail – by hand or automatically – and keep track of e-mail addresses.

Chapter Ten

Covers

E-mail explained

E-mail is short for electronic mail, and it's the Internet equivalent of letters and faxes. It's better than either, though, not only because it's quick and cheap, but also because you can attach files to an e-mail message. This means you can send text documents, pictures, sound samples and program files as well as simple messages.

You can send e-mail to anyone on the Internet; you just need to know their address, which will look something like:

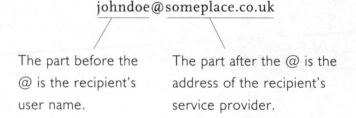

johndoe@someplace.co.uk

The part before the @ is the recipient's user name.

The part after the @ is the address of the recipient's service provider.

When you send an e-mail message, it is delivered to the recipient's service provider very quickly – usually within a few minutes. It is then stored in the recipient's mail box until he or she next logs on and checks for new e-mail.

E-mail is very efficient if you're dealing with someone who checks their mail box regularly, but not so good for getting messages to people who only log on once a week. It's also handy for contacting people who are perpetually on the phone or out of the office, and it makes it easier to deal with people in different time zones – rather than calling at an awkward hour, you can have a message waiting for them when they arrive at work.

Introducing Outlook Express

Outlook Express is a cut-down version of the Outlook application included with Microsoft Office. It doesn't have the original program's calendar, task scheduling, journal or notes sections, but it offers additional features for accessing e-mail and newsgroups (see Chapter 11). If you didn't get it with your copy of Internet Explorer, you can download it from Microsoft's Web site – see page 94 for details.

HANDY TIP

If you can't run Outlook Express from Internet Explorer, go to View>Internet Options. Click the Programs tab and make sure 'Mail:' is set to 'Outlook Express'.

1 To run Outlook Express, click the Start button and select Programs>Internet Explorer>Outlook Express. You can also run it from Internet Explorer. Click the Mail button and select Read Mail, or select Read Mail from the Go menu.

2 If you didn't fill in your e-mail details when you installed Internet Explorer, the Internet Connection Wizard may prompt you to do so (see pages 20–2).

3 You're then asked to select a connection. Choose 'Don't dial...' so you can explore the Outlook Express window.

HANDY TIP

To specify whether Outlook Express should connect to the Internet when you run it, go to Tools>Options and click the Dial Up tab. Select one of the three options.

Folder list – folders for incoming, outgoing, sent, deleted and draft messages. Click a folder to display its contents.

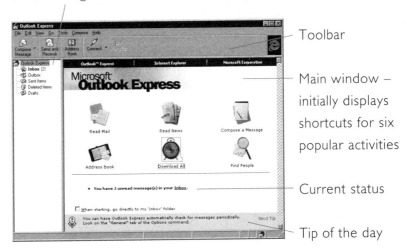

Toolbar

Main window – initially displays shortcuts for six popular activities

Current status

Tip of the day

Sending e-mail

You have to be connected to the Internet to send a message, but you don't have to be on-line while you compose it. It's best to write your messages before you log on, then send them all in a batch. You can collect any new messages at the same time (see page 146).

1 To compose a message, click the Compose Message button, select New Message from the Compose menu or press Ctrl+N.

2 A New Message window appears.

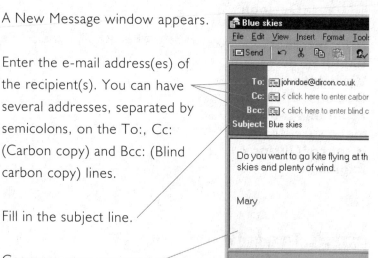

You can send mail to yourself – just enter your own address in the To: line. This is handy when you're trying out the various options.

3 Enter the e-mail address(es) of the recipient(s). You can have several addresses, separated by semicolons, on the To:, Cc: (Carbon copy) and Bcc: (Blind carbon copy) lines.

4 Fill in the subject line.

5 Compose your message.

HANDY TIP
If you have Microsoft Word or Excel, you can spellcheck your message. Select Check Spelling from the Tools menu or press F7.

6 Click the Send button (Send), select File>Send Message or press Alt+S. Confusingly, this doesn't actually send the message, it just transfers it to the Outbox. A warning message reminds that you still have to dispatch your e-mail.

...contd

7 When you're ready to send all your messages, click Send and Receive, select Tools>Send and Receive or press Ctrl+M.

8 Outlook Express connects to the Internet and sends everything in your Outbox.

Sending e-mail from the Web

Many Web pages have special links which enable you to send e-mail to their authors. Look for an underlined name or e-mail address, a 'send mail' message or a picture of an envelope or postbox.

Turn to page 68 to find out more about the *New Scientist* Web site.

1 If you hold the mouse pointer over one of these special links, you'll see an address beginning with mailto: in the Status bar.

2 Click the link to send an e-mail. The New Message window pops on to your screen, with the address already filled in. Follow the instructions opposite to complete and send the message.

Formatted e-mail

Outlook Express enables you to use HTML commands to produce e-mail messages which look as good as Web pages. This can be handy when you're trying to catch someone's eye, but it's only a good idea if you're sure they use an e-mail program which can receive formatted messages. If not, stick to plain text.

To specify which setting should be used by default, go to Tools>Options and click the Send tab. Select 'HTML' or 'Plain text'.

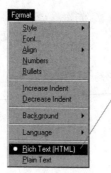

1 Use the New Message window's Format menu to switch between Rich Text (HTML) and Plain Text. A formatting bar appears when Rich Text is selected.

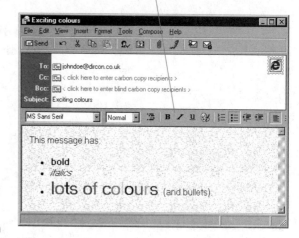

2 Use the drop-down lists and buttons to format your text. You can also use the Format menu to add background colours and images. Use the Insert menu for lines or pictures.

You can also select stationery by clicking the arrow by the Compose button.

3 There's also some built-in stationery with preselected images and colour schemes. To use it, go to Compose> New Message Using, then select a design.

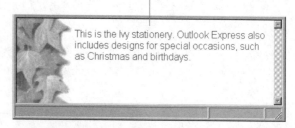

This is the Ivy stationery. Outlook Express also includes designs for special occasions, such as Christmas and birthdays.

Signatures

A signature is a short piece of text which is automatically appended to the end of every message you send. If you're sending messages from work, it might include your contact details; otherwise you could use a personal comment or favourite quote. Keep it short, though – long ones soon become tedious.

HANDY TIP

You can also set a default stationery design. Go to Tools> Stationery and click the Mail tab, then select 'This stationery'. Click the Select button to choose a design.

1 To set up a signature, go to Tools>Stationery and click the Mail tab, then click the Signature button.

2 Select 'Add this signature...'

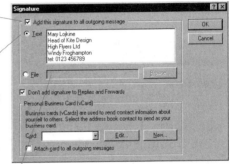

3 Select 'Text' and enter the text which is to appear at the end of your messages.

4 Alternatively, you can use your word processor to create a text (.txt) file, then select 'File' and enter the details.

5 Click OK twice to finish.

BEWARE

Don't include your personal phone number or home address in your signature unless you only send messages to people you know.

6 The text is added to the end of each message you send.

> Hi Joe, hope all's going well in the string business. I'd like to order another 1000m reel, please – the usual stuff.
>
> Mary Lojkine
> Head of Kite Design
> High Flyers Ltd
> Windy Froghampton
> tel: 0123 456789

Receiving e-mail

Unlike 'real' mail, e-mail messages aren't automatically delivered to your door – or in this case, computer. When someone sends you an e-mail, it's delivered to your service provider's mail server, which puts it into your personal mail box. You must then log on and collect it.

1 To check your mail, run Outlook Express and click Send and Receive. It will connect to the Internet (if necessary), send any messages which are waiting in your Outbox and fetch any new mail. The new messages are placed in your Inbox. You can then log off and read them at your leisure.

2 Select the Inbox folder to see a list of the messages you have received.

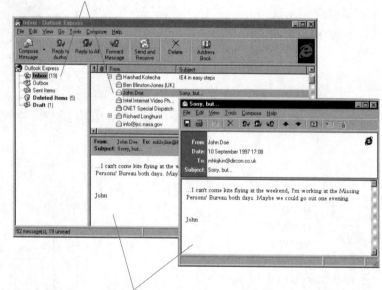

3 Click once on a message to select it and display the text in the Preview pane at the bottom of the window, or twice to display it in a separate window.

Replying and forwarding

It's easy to reply to an e-mail message, because Outlook Express automatically adds the correct address.

1 To reply to a message, select it, then click the Reply to Author button (if you've opened the message in a separate window, use the button). Alternatively, select Reply to Author from the Compose menu or press Ctrl+R. Internet Explorer opens a New Message window.

If you don't want Outlook Express to quote the previous message, select Options from the Tools menu and click on the Send tab. Deselect 'Include message in reply'.

2 The To: and Subject: lines are already filled in, and the text from the previous message is quoted at the bottom.

3 Type your reply at the top, then delete any superfluous material from the bottom section.

4 Follow steps 6–8 on pages 142–3 to send the message.

Forwarding messages

You can also divert an e-mail message to a third party.

1 To forward a message, open it and click the Forward button, select Forward from the Compose menu or press Ctrl+F. Enter the new address in the To: line.

2 Follow steps 3 and 4 above to add any comments you wish to make and send the message.

Attachments

You can also e-mail pictures and document files to your friends and colleagues. This is handy if you're working from home or collaborating on a report.

1 Compose your message (see page 142), then click the Attach File (📎) button. Alternatively, select File Attachment from the New Message window's Insert menu.

2 Find the file you want to send and click Attach. Repeat as necessary.

3 The file is added to message, which can then be sent as usual.

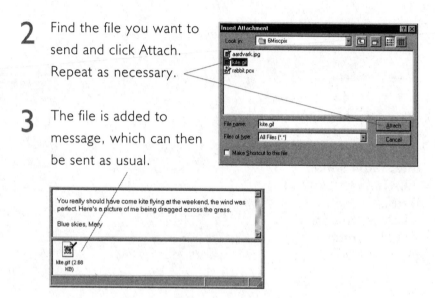

4 When you receive a message with an attached file, you'll see paperclip icons in the message list and preview pane. In some cases – for example, when a .gif or .jpg image has been attached – the file is displayed at the end of the text.

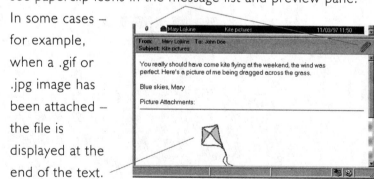

...contd

BEWARE

If you receive an attached file from someone you don't know (or don't trust), follow the instructions in step 6 to save it on to your hard disk and check for viruses before you open it (see page 105).

5 If Outlook Express hasn't displayed the file, click on the gold paperclip for more information. Click on the filename to open the attached file in a suitable application.

6 Alternatively, open the message in its own window (see page 146). You'll see an icon for the attached file at the end. Right-click on it to bring up a menu which enables you to open, print, save or view the file.

As long as the other person has the appropriate software for viewing it, you can attach pretty much any type of file, although attaching very large files may cause problems. You may also find that people who use older e-mail software cannot receive attached files.

Organising your e-mail

You can replace the folder list with an icon bar. Go to View>Layout, deselect 'Folder list' and select 'Outlook bar' instead.

Initially you have five e-mail folders: Inbox, Outbox, Sent Items, Deleted Items and Drafts.

1 New e-mail is deposited in the Inbox (see page 146).

2 Outgoing e-mail waits in the Outbox (see page 142).

3 Once a message has been dispatched, it is moved to the Sent Items folder so you have a copy.

If you're quite sure you've finished with a message, you can switch to the Deleted Items folder and delete it again. This time it will be deleted permanently.

4 If you select a message and click Delete, select Edit> Delete or press Ctrl+D, it ends up in the Deleted Items folder. You can rescue it if necessary.

5 If you close a message without sending it, Outlook Express asks if you want to save it. If you click Yes, it is moved to the Drafts folder so you can work on it again later.

Sorting your e-mail

As well as placing your e-mail in these folders, Outlook Express enables you to sort the messages in each folder.

To sort the messages in a folder, click one of the grey category tabs at the top of the list. Click again to reverse the sort. The grey triangle indicates the current sort tab.

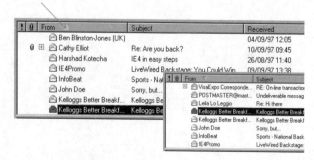

Creating your own folders

Some messages can be thrown away as soon as you've read them, but there'll be others you want to keep. You can create additional e-mail folders and file them away tidily.

1 To create a new e-mail folder, select File>Folder> New Folder.

2 Enter a name.

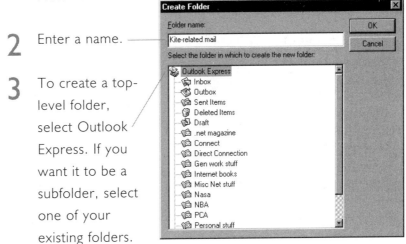

3 To create a top-level folder, select Outlook Express. If you want it to be a subfolder, select one of your existing folders.

4 The folder is added to the folder list.

5 To move messages into the folder, drag them on to it with the mouse. Alternatively, select them (hold down Shift or Ctrl to select several at once) and use Edit>Move to Folder. Select the folder and click OK.

Address Book

As you might expect, the Address Book enables you to store all the e-mail addresses you use regularly. You can then add them to messages more easily.

I   To open the Address Book, click the Address Book button, select Tools>Address Book or press Ctrl+Shift+B.

2   To add an address, click the New Contact button, select File>New Contact or press Ctrl+N.

It's even easier to add the address of someone who has sent you an e-mail message. Open the message in a separate window, then select Tools> Add to Address Book>Sender.

3   Fill in the person's name.

4   Enter a short but easy-to-remember nickname.

5   Enter the e-mail address and click Add to add it to the list. Repeat as necessary if they have several.

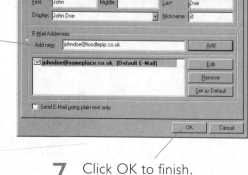

6   Click the Home, Business and Other tabs to add any other information you wish to record.

7   Click OK to finish.

8   You can now enter the person's name or nickname in the To: line of your messages. Outlook Express will look up the address when you send the message. Alternatively, click the index card icon (⊞) at the left-hand end of the To: line to choose from a list.

Searching for e-mail addresses

If you don't know someone's e-mail address, the easiest way to find it out is by asking them. If that isn't practical, you may be able to track them down using one of the on-line directories. These are a lot like phone books (they are sometimes called 'White Pages'), except they contain e-mail addresses rather than phone numbers.

1 Select Edit>Find People to search for an e-mail address. You can also do this from the Start menu, using Start>Find>People.

2 Choose an address service.

3 Enter the person's name and click Find Now.

4 Your computer will connect to the Internet and search the selected database, then display the bottom half of the dialogue box. With luck you'll see a list of names and be able to guess which one belongs to the person you are looking for.

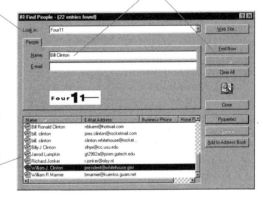

5 If you don't succeed, try one of the other services – they all have different databases.

6 You might also like to visit the Web pages of the various services (just click the Web site button) and register your details so your friends can look you up.

Inbox Assistant

The Inbox Assistant is your personal mail clerk. It can be taught to file, delete or reply to many of your incoming messages, leaving you more time for the important ones.

The Assistant works by following a set of rules which tell it what to look for, and what to do when it finds a particular pattern. You have to tell it how to do this, though, so start by taking a look at the e-mail in your Inbox and deciding how it should be treated.

1   Summon the Assistant using Tools > Inbox Assistant.

2   Click the Add button to create your first rule.

3   Enter a pattern in the top section. Here the Inbox Assistant is to look for messages from John Doe.

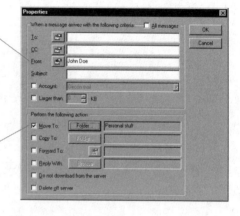

4   Enter an action in the bottom section. In this case, the message is to be moved to the 'Personal stuff' folder.

5   Click OK.

HANDY TIP

The rules are applied in order, so make sure the most important ones are at the top. Click Move Up and Move Down to reorganise them.

6   Your new rule is added to the list. Repeat steps 2–5 to create as many rules as you need.

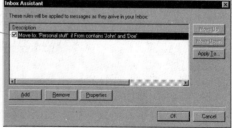

7   All your incoming mail will be sorted according to the rules you've created.

Multiple accounts

Outlook Express can be set up to handle several e-mail accounts. You might need this facility if you have separate accounts for business and private e-mail, or if several people use the same computer to access their mail.

1 To add a new account, select Tools>Accounts. Click the Mail tab, then click Add and select Mail.

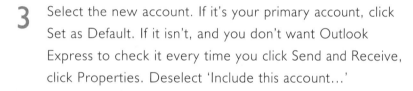

2 The Connection Wizard helps you enter your details (see pages 20–2).

The default account is used when you click the Send button. Unless you specify otherwise (see step 3), *all* your accounts are checked when you click Send and Receive.

3 Select the new account. If it's your primary account, click Set as Default. If it isn't, and you don't want Outlook Express to check it every time you click Send and Receive, click Properties. Deselect 'Include this account...'

4 To send a message using a particular account, select Send Message Using from the Message window's File menu, then choose one of your accounts.

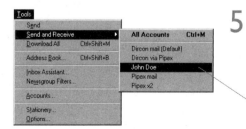

5 To check for messages in a particular mailbox, go to Tools>Send and Receive and select the account.

Making the most of e-mail

E-mail isn't just a way to bypass the postbox and fax machine. It also enables you to keep informed, join discussion groups, play games and have some fun with your friends.

The easiest way to fill your Inbox is by subscribing to a few mailing lists. There are two sorts: announcement lists, which deliver regular newsletter-style messages, and discussion lists, which are more like e-mail conversations. Everyone on the list submits their news, thoughts, recipes or whatever to the mail server, which copies them to all the members. They're a good way to get in touch with Internet users who share your interests.

Many of the bigger Web sites have announcement lists which tell you what has been added each week. You can usually sign up somewhere on the site – in fact you'll often find that registering (see page 82) puts you on the list. Discussion lists may also have associated Web pages, but you usually sign up by e-mail. The best place to start is the Liszt Web site, which provides details of over 70,000 mailing lists. Find it at:

`http://www.liszt.com/`

Play-by-e-mail games are also popular. You can play almost anything, including board, strategy and role-playing games, or join a fantasy sports league. Some work entirely by e-mail – you simply submit your move and wait for a response – while others take moves by e-mail, then display the results on a Web site.

Finally, there are lots of Web sites which use e-mail to deliver useful or amusing services. You can send electronic postcards to your friends, use automatic letter-writers to generate romantic or sarcastic messages, or even order a (picture of a) pizza over the Web. On a more practical note, you can also sign up for reminder services which send you messages on (or just before) important dates such as birthdays and anniversaries.

Usenet newsgroups

Usenet newsgroups enable you to communicate with Internet users who share your interests. This chapter shows you how to read and post messages, then explains newsgroup etiquette and customs.

Chapter Eleven

Covers

Newsgroups explained

The Usenet newsgroups are the Internet equivalent of your local pub or social club. They're nowhere near as pretty as the Web, but they're more interactive. If you're looking for gossip, trivia, advice, arguments and – very occasionally – news, Usenet is the place to find it.

 Newsgroup 'messages' are also referred to as 'posts' and 'articles'. The three terms are interchangeable.

A newsgroup is essentially a public mail box dedicated to a particular topic. Anyone on the Internet can post a message, and anyone else can read it and upload a reply.

Unlike Web pages, newsgroups exist in more than one place. All the messages are regularly copied from one news server to another, enabling you to access them locally. Rather than connecting to lots of sites from all over the globe, you download the latest messages from your service provider's news server.

There are over 30,000 newsgroups to choose from, although some service providers only carry the more popular ones. Some have a close-knit community of regular posters; others are larger and more anonymous. Either way, though, there's certain to be someone who wants to share your experiences, answer your questions, ask for advice or just pass the time of day.

Understanding newsgroup names

Newsgroup addresses look like:
`rec.arts.movies.reviews`

or sometimes:
`news:rec.arts.movies.reviews`

Newsgroups are organised hierarchically: each section of the address (moving from left to right) reduces the scope of the group. In this case `rec` stands for recreation, `arts` and `movies` are self-evident and the group only carries `reviews`. There are ten other `movies` groups, about 100 other `arts` groups, and over 500 `rec` groups in total.

`rec` is only one of dozens of top-level categories. However, you can find almost everything you're likely to want in `alt`, `comp`, `news`, `rec`, `sci`, `soc` and `uk`.

alt (alternative)

Almost anyone can create an `alt` newsgroup, so the `alt` hierarchy is one of the liveliest sections of Usenet. Some of the groups are pretty wild, but most are just odd – if you're interested in alien conspiracies, urban legends or breakfast cereal (no, really), `alt` has much to offer. It's also a nursery for new groups, some of which eventually graduate to the more respectable hierarchies.

comp (computing)

The `comp` groups deal with everything from hardware and software to artificial intelligence and home automation.

news (Usenet)

The `news` groups are for discussion about Usenet. They aren't terribly exciting, but `news.announce.newusers` has lots of information for beginners.

rec (recreation)

The `rec` groups cover hobbies, sports, arts and music, and are the best place to start. They tend to be friendlier than the `alt` groups and are easy to find your way around.

sci (science)

The `sci` groups cover mathematics, physics, engineering, chemistry, biological science, medicine, psychology and philosophy – everything except computing, basically.

soc (social)

The `soc` groups deal with social issues. The biggest subsection, `soc.culture`, has well over 100 groups dedicated to various countries and cultures. Genealogy, history and religion are well represented, and there are a number of support groups.

uk (United Kingdom)

The `uk` groups are a microcosm of Usenet as a whole. The most popular groups are `uk.politics` and `uk.misc`, but you'll also find job ads, an *Archers* group and a selection of `rec` and `religion` groups.

Getting started

There are many similarities between sending e-mail and posting messages to newsgroups. You use the same application – Outlook Express – for both, and many operations are identical. However, you will notice some changes in the menus when you switch from sending and receiving e-mail to reading news.

If you didn't get Outlook Express with your copy of Internet Explorer, you can download it from Microsoft's Web site – see page 94 for details.

HANDY TIP

If you can't run Outlook Express from Internet Explorer, go to View>Internet Options. Click the Programs tab and make sure 'News:' is set to 'Outlook Express'.

1 To run Outlook Express, click the Start button and select Programs>Internet Explorer>Outlook Express. You can also run it from Internet Explorer. Click the Mail button and select Read News, or select News from the Go menu.

2 If you didn't provide details of your service provider's news server when you installed Internet Explorer, the Connection Wizard may prompt you to do so (see pages 20–2).

3 The first thing you need to do is download the list of available newsgroups. If you've just entered your details, you'll be prompted to do so; otherwise select your news server from the folder list and click the Newsgroups button or select Tools>Newsgroups.

4 Outlook Express connects to the Internet and downloads the newsgroup list. This takes a few minutes, but you only have to do it once.

...contd

Subscrib-ing to a newsgroup isn't like subscribing to a magazine or club. You don't have to pay anything, and you won't be added to a membership list. Subscribing simply tells Outlook Express that you're interested in particular groups.

5 The newsgroup list appears. You now need to select some newsgroups and 'subscribe' to them.

6 Scroll down the list until you find a group which looks interesting, then select it and click the Subscribe button. To find groups covering a particular subject, type a word which the name might contain in the 'Display...' box.

7 Click the Subscribed tab to see a list of the groups you have subscribed to. If you change your mind about a newsgroup, select it and click the Unsubscribe button.

8 If you want to subscribe to some more groups later on, click the Newsgroups button or select Tools>Newsgroups. You won't have to download the list again – Outlook Express stores it on your hard disk.

Reading news

Reading newsgroup messages is slightly different from reading e-mail. Instead of downloading all the messages, which might take some time, Outlook Express only fetches the headers (the subject line, name of sender and so on). You can then download the ones which sound interesting.

1   Click Connect to connect to the Internet.

2   Select your news server from the folder list to display your subscribed newsgroups.

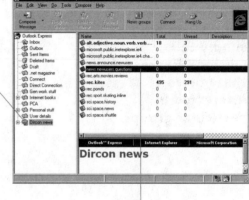

Some groups are very busy and receive hundreds of new messages each day. To tell Outlook Express how many headers to fetch, select Tools> Options and click the Read tab. Enter a number in the 'Download...' box.

3   Double-click one of the groups to download the titles of the current messages.

4   Click a title to download and display the body of the message.

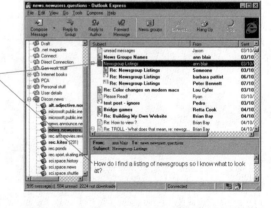

5   On-going discussions are 'threaded' – the responses are displayed immediately below the original message. Click the plus (⊞) and minus (⊟) icons to expand and contract the threads.

Working off-line

You can minimise the amount of time you spend on-line by 'marking' the messages you want to read and downloading them all at once. You can then read them at your leisure, without worrying about your phone bill.

1 Download the headers from one or more newsgroups (steps 1–3, opposite), then click Hang Up or select File>Hang Up.

2 Select the messages you want to read, then use Tools>Mark for Retrieval> Mark Message to mark them. You can also mark entire threads or newsgroups. Blue

arrows ([⌐⌐]) appear beside marked messages.

3 Select Tools>Download All to connect to the Internet and download the marked messages. Hang up again.

4 The downloaded messages can be identified by their complete ([▤]) rather than partial ([⌐]) message icons. Click their headers to display them in the preview pane.

Posting messages

Posting messages is similar to sending e-mail (see pages 142–3), but you address the message to the newsgroup.

1 To create a new message, make sure you are viewing the correct newsgroup, then click Compose Message, select Compose>New Message or press Ctrl+N.

HANDY TIP

If your response won't be of interest to anyone other than the original poster, you can e-mail it directly to them. Click Reply to Author, select Compose>Reply to Author or press Ctrl+R to create a pre-addressed form.

2 To respond to an existing message, select it, then click Reply to Group, select Compose>Reply to Newsgroup or press Ctrl+G.

3 Either way, Outlook Express brings up a pre-addressed New Message window (if you're responding to an existing message, the original text is quoted – see page 147). Fill in the Subject line and compose your message.

4 To send the message immediately, select File>Send Message.

5 If you're working off-line, click the Post button (Post), select File>Send Later or press Alt+S to transfer the message to your Outbox. Once you've composed all your messages, select Outbox from the folder list to switch to e-mail mode. Click Send and Receive or select Tools>Send and Receive to dispatch your messages.

Newsgroup filters

Newsgroup filters enable you to ignore messages from people who are being obnoxious or posting irrelevant messages. You can also filter messages by subject.

Like the Inbox Assistant (see page 154), newsgroup filters apply a set of rules to incoming messages. The options are slightly different, but the principles are the same.

1 To create a new rule, select Tools > Newsgroup Filters.

2 Click the Add button.

3 Decide whether the filter should be applied to all newsgroups, all the groups on a particular server, or just a specific group.

4 Enter the name of the person who is to be ignored, or a word which might appear in the Subject line.

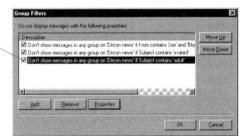

5 Your new rule is added to the list. Repeat steps 2–4 to create as many rules as you need.

6 Messages which meet any of your criteria will not be displayed.

Netiquette

Usenet has a reputation for being hostile to beginners or 'newbies'. While it's true that some groups are hard to break into, most welcome anyone who displays a little common sense and courtesy. In particular, try to adhere to the following guidelines, known collectively as 'netiquette'.

A 'flame' is an abusive message. Some groups tolerate and even encourage flaming; others expect members to be civil. If you post a flame, be prepared to get flamed back!

1   Always read the FAQ (see opposite) before you start posting messages, to avoid (a) posting messages that are inappropriate or (b) asking questions which have already been answered hundreds of times.

2   Don't post the same message to several groups at once. This is known as 'cross posting', and it irritates the people who end up downloading your message several times.

3   Don't ever post the same message to lots and lots of newsgroups. This is known as 'spamming', and it irritates everyone. Sadly, you'll encounter lots of spam on Usenet, especially in the `alt` groups. Ignore it – responding just makes things worse.

4   If you're replying to a message, don't quote more of the original than is necessary – most people won't want to read it all again. It's helpful to quote the sentence or two you're actually responding to, though.

5   Don't type your message entirely in upper case. This is known as SHOUTING, AND IT MAKES YOUR MESSAGE DIFFICULT TO READ.

FAQs

A FAQ is a compilation of Frequently Asked Questions – and their answers. FAQs exist for two reasons: to set out the newsgroup's scope and rules, and to answer all the questions a newcomer might ask.

'Lurkers' read the messages in a newsgroup, but don't post anything. This is how most people start off – it's a good way to get a feel for what is acceptable in a particular group.

Most FAQs are posted regularly, generally weekly or monthly. If you 'lurk' in a newsgroup for a while, the FAQ should eventually appear. You can also find FAQs for many newsgroups at:

`http://www.cis.ohio-state.edu/hypertext/faq/usenet/top.html`

If all else fails, post a polite message asking someone to point you in the right direction. Note that some groups don't have FAQs; others have more than one, and some FAQs serve several groups. If you can't find a FAQ, lurk for a week or two to get a feel for the group.

Many FAQs represent the collective knowledge of the members of the newsgroup, and they can be fascinating reading in their own right. The question-and-answer format has also become popular elsewhere on the Internet. Many Web sites have FAQ pages, and they're also starting to appear in printed leaflets and guides.

Smileys and acronyms

Smileys and acronyms speed things up and enable you to clarify your comments.

Smileys

HANDY TIP

Smileys are sometimes called 'emoticons'. Don't use too many – some people think they're a bit silly.

It's difficult to convey emotion in a brief text message. This can lead to misunderstandings, particularly if you tend to be blunt or sarcastic. Consequently some people use 'smileys' – little faces made out of keyboard characters – to convey their state of mind.

There are many, many smileys, but the two you're most likely to encounter are:

:-)	happy, or 'only joking'
:-(	sad or disappointed

(Turn the book through 90 degrees to see the faces.)

Acronyms

Common phrases are often abbreviated to just their initials, producing TLAs (Three-Letter Acronyms) and ETLAs (Extended TLAs). You'll also come across some phonetic abbreviations.

Common acronyms and abbreviations include:

AFAIK	As far as I know
B4	Before
BTW	By the way
F2F	Face to face
FYI	For your information
<g>	Grin
IMHO	In my humble opinion
IMNSHO	In my not so humble opinion
ISTM	It seems to me
ISTR	I seem to recall
IRL	In real life (meaning, off the Internet)
L8R	Later
ROFL	Rolling on floor laughing
RSN	Real soon now
RTFM	Read the 'flipping' manual

NetMeeting

This chapter introduces NetMeeting, a conferencing tool which enables you to hold conversations across the Internet. It shows you how to set up the software and make a call, then explains how to exchange text messages, drawings and files as you converse.

Covers

Chapter Twelve

Introducing NetMeeting

NetMeeting is a conferencing application which enables you to talk to other Internet users. It's just like chatting on the telephone, except that the sound is digitised and transmitted over the Internet. You don't get the sound quality you'd expect from a regular telephone, but you can talk to faraway friends for the cost of a local call to your service provider.

The other good thing about NetMeeting is that it can do more than a regular telephone. As well as simply talking to other users, you can send and receive video, exchange text messages and files, draw maps and diagrams on a whiteboard and work together in shared applications. These extra tools help compensate for occasional glitches in the audio. If you want to give someone a phone number, for example, you can type it into the text chat window rather than relying on them hearing you correctly. Transmitting drawings and photographs can be more effective than describing things in words, especially since – unlike a fax machine – NetMeeting sends and receives in colour.

Unless you're using NetMeeting across an internal network which can shift data more quickly than the Internet, it's no match for the videophones of the science-fiction future. That said, it works surprisingly well. You end up repeating yourself quite a lot, but it's still possible to have a coherent conversation, and the extra tools enable you to do more than just exchange gossip.

If you didn't get NetMeeting with your copy of Internet Explorer, you can download it from Microsoft's Web site – see page 94 for details.

Getting started

If you just want to type messages to other Internet users, you don't need anything special to use NetMeeting. To actually talk to them, you'll need a soundcard with a microphone and speakers or headphones. Use the Sound Recorder application supplied with Windows to check that you can record and play sounds before you try to set up NetMeeting. Finally, if you have a video camera connected to your computer, you'll also be able to send video images.

1   To run NetMeeting, click the Start button and select Programs>Internet Explorer>NetMeeting.

2   The first time you do this, the NetMeeting Wizard helps you configure the program.

3   The directory server enables you to find out who's on-line. Accept the defaults – you can change these settings later if necessary (see page 173).

4   Fill in your personal details. The things you type here will appear in your listing on the directory server.

5   The Audio Tuning Wizard then finds your soundcard and helps you choose the correct settings.

6   The device settings should be correct. On the next screen, select your connection speed.

7   Click the Start Recording button and read the sample paragraph, speaking into the microphone as you would into a telephone.

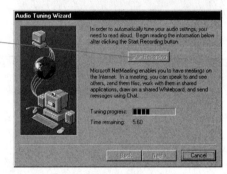

HANDY TIP   **The next time you want to run Net-Meeting, go to Start>Programs> Internet Explorer> NetMeeting. You can also run it from Internet Explorer by selecting Go> Internet Call.**

8   Click Next and Finish to run NetMeeting. It connects to the directory server and lists people who are taking calls.

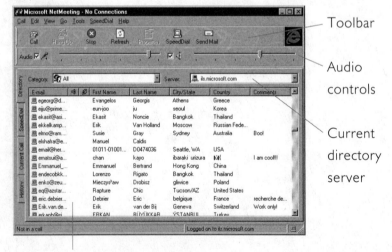

Toolbar

Audio controls

Current directory server

List of people currently logged on, showing where they are, what equipment they have and so on

The directory server

Making Internet calls is rather different from making regular telephone calls. First, whereas there's a good chance that someone will be within earshot of their telephone, few people are on-line 24 hours a day. Second, people who have dial-up connections usually get a different IP number (see page 14) each time they log on. This means you can't call your friends directly, because you don't know exactly where on the Net they are.

The directory server helps overcome both problems: it tells you who is available to take a call, and it can connect you to the address they logged on from. It's essentially a global receptionist, and logging on is the Internet equivalent of calling the switchboard and saying, 'Hi, I'm in Room 202 today, put my calls through to extension 2058.'

REMEMBER

You probably wouldn't dial a random telephone number and expect the person on the other end to be willing to chat, but Internet users make random calls all the time. It's a bit like ham radio – the objective is to talk to people from lots of other places.

Microsoft operates several directory servers. The main one is often very busy, so you might want to tell your friends to look for you on one of the others. You can also opt for the Internet equivalent of an unlisted number if you don't want to receive calls from strangers.

1   To change your default server, go to Tools > Options and click on the Calling tab.

2   Select a server.

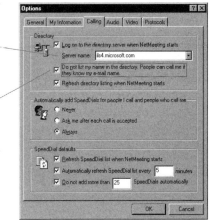

3   If you don't want your name listed, select 'Do not list...' People who know your e-mail address will still be able to call you, but you won't be bothered by strangers.

Making a call

Once you're connected to the directory server, you can either place a call or wait for someone to call you.

1   To place a call, click the Call button or select Call>New Call.

2   Enter the e-mail address of the person you want to speak to and click Call.

3   Alternatively, scan down the directory server list and double-click the person's entry.

4   To receive a call, wait for your computer to 'ring', then click Accept.

5   Once you've made the connection, you can start talking. If you have a camera, select Tools>Video> Send to send images as well as sound.

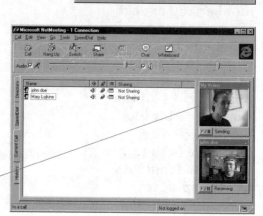

6   To end the call, click the Hang Up button or select Call>Hang Up.

Using the tools

You can transmit text messages, files or pictures as you talk. If you're sending video, it's a good idea to pause it before you try to use any of the other tools.

Chat

The Chat window is useful when you're having problems with your audio. You can also use it to conduct typed conversations with people who don't have soundcards.

You can only exchange audio and video with one person at a time. If you use the Chat window instead, several people can converse together.

1. Go to Tools>Chat to open the Chat window. The other person's window should open automatically.

2. Type your message in the bottom section of the window, then click the button to send it. All the messages are displayed at the top, in the order they were sent.

Whiteboard

The Whiteboard enables you to exchange images.

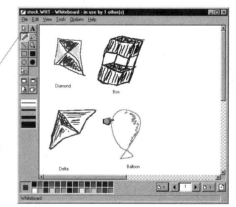

1. Select Tools> Whiteboard to open the Whiteboard.

2. Use the drawing tools to create maps and diagrams. You can also type labels and messages.

3. To send a photograph, open it in a suitable application, then select and copy it. Use Edit>Paste to place it on the Whiteboard.

File transfer

You can also dispatch files while you converse. This is the easiest way to exchange photographs.

1 To send a file, go to Tools>File Transfer>Send File.

2 Select the file and click Send. You'll see a 'Sending file' message at the left-hand end of the NetMeeting Status bar.

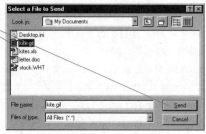

3 Any files you receive end up in a special folder which can be accessed using Tools> File Transfer>Open Received Files Folder.

Application sharing

Sharing an application enables you to show someone a spreadsheet or document. You can also work together, taking turns with the mouse.

1 To share an application, open it, then go to Tools>Share Application and select it from the submenu.

2 A grey tab in the corner indicates that both parties can see the window. Only you can work in it...

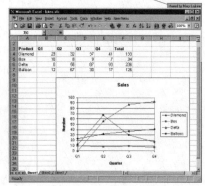

3 ...until you select Tools> Start Collaborating. A label by the mouse pointer shows who has control. Click the mouse to take your turn.

Chapter Thirteen

FrontPage Express

This chapter explains how to create your own Web pages with FrontPage Express. It shows you how to enter and format text, insert images and create links to produce a simple Web site. It then introduces some of the more advanced features, including scrolling messages and tables. Finally, it explains how to publish your pages on your service provider's Web server.

Covers

Introducing FrontPage Express

FrontPage Express enables you to create Web pages without mastering the inner workings of HTML (see page 33). Instead of placing all the tags by hand, you use menus and toolbars to format the text on your page, insert pictures and links and so on. It's like using a modern word processor – you can see how the finished page will look, and you keep experimenting until you're happy with the layout. FrontPage Express then saves the page in a format Web browsers can understand.

If you didn't get FrontPage Express with your copy of Internet Explorer, you can download it from Microsoft's Web site – see page 94 for details.

HANDY TIP

You can also run FrontPage Express from Internet Explorer, by clicking the Edit button or selecting Edit> Page. Either action transfers the page you're viewing to FrontPage Express, which is handy if you come across an interesting layout and want to see how it was created.

1   To run FrontPage Express, click the Start button and select Programs>Internet Explorer>FrontPage Express.

2   The FrontPage Express window appears, displaying a new (blank) Web page.

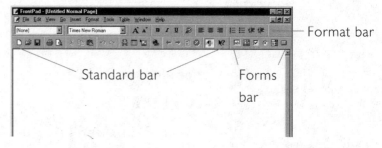

Standard bar   Forms bar   Format bar

Although FrontPage Express does its best to make Web design painless, to get the best out of it you need to understand how it works, which means learning about HTML. If the material in this chapter whets your appetite, look out for three of the other books in this series, *HTML in easy steps*, *Web Page Design in easy steps* and *FrontPage in easy steps*, which provide a lot more information.

Entering the text

Entering and formatting the text is the easiest part of creating a Web page. You don't have as many options as word processors provide, but the procedures are similar.

1   It's very important to keep all your Web page files together, so create a new folder for them before you start.

2   Enter all your text.

3   Use the Format bar to style selected words or paragraphs.

HANDY TIP

Your fonts will only be used if the person viewing the page has them installed on their computer. It's best to stick to Arial, Courier New, Comic Sans, Impact, Times New Roman and Verdana.

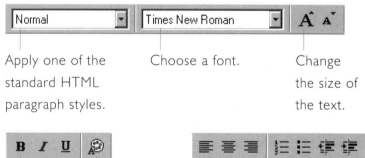

Apply one of the standard HTML paragraph styles.

Choose a font.

Change the size of the text.

Apply bold, italics or underlining.

Change the text colour.

Align the paragraphs.

Add numbers, bullets or indents.

REMEMBER

Limit the filename to eight characters. Don't include upper-case letters, spaces or other unusual characters.

4   Click Save (![save]) or select File > Save to save the page. Give your Web page a title.

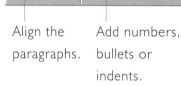

5   At this stage it's best to save it on your hard disk, so click As File. Give the file a meaningful name and save it into the folder you created in step 1.

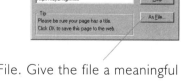

Inserting images

A text-only Web page is unlikely to attract much attention, so insert some images to liven things up. As well as simply illustrating the text, image files can be used to add logos, bullets, buttons and backgrounds.

 HANDY TIP

You can download lots of useful images from the Gallery section of Microsoft's Site Builder Network. Find it at:
`http://www.microsoft.com/gallery/`

1 Use a graphics program to create your image. Save it as a .gif (drawings and logos) or .jpg (photographs) file. Put it in the same folder as your Web page (see previous page).

2 Position the cursor where you want the image to appear. Click the Image button (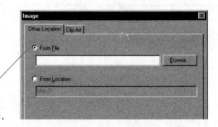) or select Insert> Image. Click the Other Location tab and select 'From file', then click Browse to locate your file.

3 The image is added to your page. You can use the paragraph-formatting buttons to align it – click on it to select it, then click Align Left, Centre or Align Right.

4 For more advanced formatting commands, select the image, then select Edit>Image Properties.

If you don't want a white background, you can change the colour or replace it with an image. Go to Format> Background and select an image or colour.

Creating links

Once you've designed two or three pages, you'll want to link them together. You may also want to insert links which lead to pages elsewhere on the Web.

You *must* keep all your files in a single folder, or in sub-folders within that folder, if you want everything to work properly when you upload your pages to the Web (see page 185).

1. To link two of your own pages, open them both in FrontPage Express.

2. Use the Window menu to switch to the page you want to link from. Select the text or image which will 'anchor' the link, then click the Hyperlink button (📖), select Insert> Hyperlink or press Ctrl+K.

3. Click the Open Pages tab, select the page you want to link to and click OK. Ignore the warning message.

4. To link to a page on the Web, open it in Internet Explorer. Switch back to FrontPage Express and repeat step 2 to create the anchor.

If you know the address of the page you want to link to, you don't need to open it – just type the address into the dialogue box.

5. Click the World Wide Web tab. You should see the address of the page you've opened in Internet Explorer. Click OK to create the link.

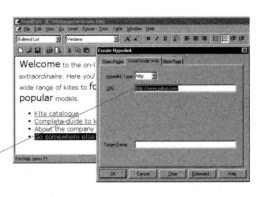

Other elements

You can supplement your text and images with everything from horizontal lines to background sounds and scrolling messages. All these 'extras' are found in the Insert menu.

1 To break a paragraph without adding any space between the two sections, select Insert>Break.

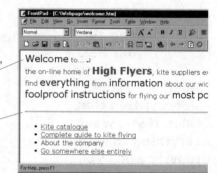

2 To draw a line across the page, select Insert> Horizontal Line.

3 The Insert>WebView commands are useful when you're creating Web pages for your folders (see page 131).

4 To add a video clip or sound file, select Insert> Video or Insert> Background Sound. These files should be kept in the same folder as your pages, images and so on.

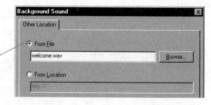

5 To add a scrolling message, select Insert>Marquee. Enter the message text.

6 Open the page in Internet Explorer (select File>Open, then click Browse to locate the file) to see how the marquee looks. To adjust any of the parameters, return to FrontPage Express, select the marquee and go to Edit>Properties.

Tables

Tables enable you to create more sophisticated pages. They're used to create layouts with several columns of text, or where text and images need to be arranged precisely.

1 Select Table>Insert Table to create a new table.

To change the table settings later on, click in any cell and select Table>Table Properties.

2 Specify the number of cells.

3 Specify the text alignment.

4 Set the thickness of the cell outlines (zero turns them off).

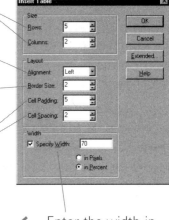

5 Set the amount of space between the text and the border (Padding) and between adjacent cells (Spacing).

6 Enter the width in pixels or per cent.

If you don't enter a width, the size of the table depends on the size of the browser window and the length of the longest entry in each column.

7 Click OK to add the table to your page.

8 Type your text into the table cells, which expand as required.

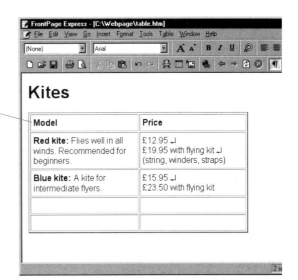

...contd

HANDY TIP

Once you've selected one cell using Table>Select Cell, you can extend the selection by pressing Shift and clicking other cells. The selected cells don't have to be adjacent.

9 To change the formatting of a cell or group of cells, select it/them using Table>Select Cell, then go to Table> Cell Properties. You can change the text alignment, background and border colours and cell width.

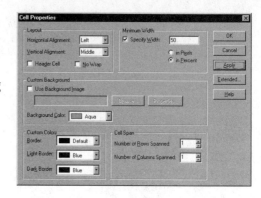

10 To join two or more cells together, select them and use Table>Merge Cells.

Model	Price
Red kite: Flies well in all winds. Recommended for beginners.	£12.95 ↵ £19.95 with flying kit ↵ (string, winders, straps)
Blue kite: A kite for intermediate flyers.	£15.95 ↵ £23.50 with flying kit
Green kite: A high-tech kite for expert flyers. Light to medium winds only.	£49.95
All prices include packing, postage and VAT.	

11 To add cells, use Table>Insert Row or Column.

HANDY TIP

Set the borders to zero (see step 4) for a more informal layout. The table will keep your pictures and text aligned, but the structure of the page won't be as obvious.

12 You can also insert images. Position the cursor in a cell, then select Insert>Image (see page 180).

The Web Publishing Wizard

If you want other Internet users to be able to view your pages, you need to copy them on to a Web server – a computer which is permanently connected to the Internet and set up to 'serve' Web pages. Most service providers let each member store 1–5Mb of files in a personal folder on one of their servers. You can use this space to 'publish' your Web pages.

The Web Publishing Wizard helps you copy your files on to a Web server. You'll need to ask your service provider for the address of your folder before you can do this.

Before you upload your Web pages, open all the files in Internet Explorer and check that everything looks right and works correctly.

1 To run the Web Publishing Wizard, click Start and select Programs>Internet Explorer>Web Publishing Wizard.

2 Enter the name of the folder which you saved your pages into (see page 179), or click Browse Folders to find it.

3 Enter a name for the server. Next time you publish your pages you'll be able to select this name instead of entering all the details.

4 Enter the address
of the folder
where your pages
are kept. Do *not*
add a slash (/) at
the end – the
Wizard will get
confused.

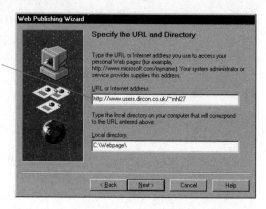

5 The Wizard will then
connect to the Internet
and try to find this folder.
You may be prompted
for a user name and
password. These will
probably be the same as the ones you use to log on.

HANDY TIP

If the Web Publishing Wizard gives you an error message, contact your service provider for advice. You may need to upload your pages some other way.

6 Click Finish to copy your
pages from the folder on
your hard disk to the
folder on the Web server.

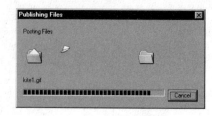

7 You can now use Internet
Explorer to browse your pages. Enter the name of the
folder, followed by the name of a file, in the Address bar.

Index